NO ORDINARY JOB

A MEMOIR OF WORKING IN THE SASKATCHEWAN HOSPITAL NORTH BATTLEFORD IN THE 1950'S

Edward Skalazub

Table of Contents

Preface	**v**
Chapter 1 *Is It Always So Cold?*	**1**
Chapter 2 *Someone Who Had No Choice*	**7**
Chapter 3 *Giving a Hand*	**12**
Chapter 4 *Lifelong Friends*	**18**
Chapter 5 *The Watchfuls*	**22**
Chapter 6 *Built To Last*	**28**
Chapter 7 *Money Well Spent*	**31**
Chapter 8 *Remember This*	**36**
Chapter 9 *Could More Have Been Done?*	**42**
Chapter 10 *A Broken Reed*	**48**
Chapter 11 *Out In the World*	**51**
Chapter 12 *All This For Nothing*	**55**
Chapter 13 *The Elopers*	**59**
Chapter 14 *The Wrong House*	**67**
Chapter 15 *Shanghai*	**77**

Chapter 16   **84**
A Narrow Escape

Chapter 17   **89**
They're Not Crazy

Chapter 18   **92**
Messiah God King

Chapter 19   **98**
Something a Man Couldn't Do

Chapter 20   **101**
Disgusting Creatures

Chapter 21   **105**
Is That Clock Right?

Chapter 22   **108**
Leave That Up To the Old Man

Afterword   **113**

| No Ordinary Job

Preface

It was 1952, the middle of one of the coldest winters Saskatchewan had experienced, and I was to begin a period in my life that I never would have imagined. In desperation I had been forced to begin working at the Saskatchewan Hospital in North Battleford (SHNB). It was what was called a mental hospital in those days; the term psychiatric hospital was certainly not in the vocabulary of anyone I knew.

Little did I know that what was meant to be a temporary emergency measure would lead to events and experiences that would mark my life more than anything else I might have done and would affect my future like nothing else.

Since leaving home under rather hurried circumstances at the age of sixteen I had lived a life that might be considered somewhat adventurous. I had held a variety of jobs, I had sailed the Great Lakes and the Great Oceans, had been in shipwrecks, and faced the possibility of being sunk in a North Pacific gale. I had married young in New Zealand and spent three years of my life in that beautiful land. Circumstances had plunged me into shameful episodes of labour strife and monumental injustices both in this country and overseas. Yet, in years to come all this was to recede into insignificance. It was the years at SHNB that were to fill my thoughts and dreams.

| No Ordinary Job

Chapter 1

Is It Always So Cold?

Why the train stopped so far from the station in Edmonton we never did find out. As we stepped down from the car the intense cold literally took our breath away. Clara gasped, and even I, who had grown up in the prairies, was taken aback. A long line of bundled-up figures trudged down a single path of packed snow toward a distant cluster of lights, obviously the station. Clara and I, in our summer-weight clothing, bareheaded and barehanded, joined the stream. Within minutes we were shivering – our teeth chattering. Allan, our five-month-old, totally covered up in his carrycot, slept on. Fortunately, our larger baggage was checked through. I toted the carrycot with its precious cargo; Clara the diaper bag. These we switched from hand to hand, our free hand alternately seeking the warmth of a pocket and giving our stinging ears and noses a quick rub. When we finally walked through the doors into the cavernous waiting room we were on our last legs. All we could do was flop down on the hard, uncomfortable wooden bench and try to recover our strength and courage. Although it was near midnight the lunch counter was still open and hot tea soon restored us to life.

"Is it always so cold?" asked Clara, no doubt already regretting her decision to leave her homeland. Just the night before she had exclaimed over her first sight of snow. Later we found out that we had arrived in the middle of a record-breaking cold spell, with temperatures dropping as low as sixty degrees below zero Fahrenheit.

We were in the last stages of a journey that was to take us from mid-summer New Zealand to the frigid heart of Canada. Three years before I had left my ship in New Zealand with every intention of leaving Canada forever. I had been moved to do so by one of the most shameful episodes in Canadian history: the seamen's lockout of the late 40's when a Canadian government, anxious to out-McCarthy McCarthy turned a gang of American hoodlums loose against decent Canadian workers. Having visited New Zealand on previous voyages I considered it a paradise with its friendly, welcoming people, zero unemployment and a social safety net that included medicare and free education to all levels. On a previous voyage I had met a New Zealand girl and we were married not long after my arrival. But in the same year, 1949, the Labour government was defeated after almost twenty years in power. A vengeful conservative party set out to try to undo many of the advances of the previous twenty years. The union of which I was a member was forced out on strike for half a year. Social groups were pitted against each other. Disillusioned, I decided to return to Canada.

So it was that on a January night in 1952 we set out on the Wellington-Auckland Express, a twelve-hour test of endurance. The following day we boarded the venerable trans-Pacific liner Aorangi as third-class passengers. It was the last trip for the Aorangi, which was being retired after decades of service, including war-time service as a troopship. It turned out to be a fortunate circumstance for us as, due to mechanical problems, what should have been a two-week voyage turned into a half-speed tropical cruise of almost double that time. We had stops in Fiji and Honolulu. At both ports we were able to take our distinctive baby carriage ashore and this never failed to excite interest among the locals. At a market in Suva, a large Fijian lady said, "Leave him with me. I'll soon fatten him up." In Honolulu a friendly matron stopped to talk. Looking at him she remarked, "If he lived here he wouldn't be so pale." After hearing about our trip and what remained of it she said, "Go into that store and buy some paper napkins." We had never heard of such a thing but, sure enough, there they were and on sale too. In spite of our limited resources we bought a few dozen and they turned out to be a godsend; their availability made the remainder of the journey, especially the rail portion, so much easier. Those "disposables" were nothing like the scientific marvels we have today. They were simply what they claimed to be: napkins made of thick, absorbent paper, but they certainly served the purpose for which they were designed.

One day out of Honolulu and we had to accept the fact that we were leaving the tropics behind. Jackets and sweaters began to appear on deck and the glorious sun was now shrouded in cloud for a good part of the day. Soon it was no longer seen, as typical west coast winter weather took over. We arrived in Vancouver on the second day of February on a reasonably nice day for Vancouver: grey, no sun, but also, no rain. Our train for Edmonton did not leave until near midnight so we had time to walk around the city. Our limited budget did not allow for any shopping and we had a long, uncomfortable wait at the train station. It was a relief to finally board the train and find our berths. We had been able to prepay our tickets, including sleepers, before we left New Zealand.

The wait in Edmonton was not as lengthy and soon we were on our way to our final destination – Radisson, Saskatchewan. Radisson's population, of about 400 persons, qualified it to have a solid black dot on the provincial map. Eight years before, a restless and defiant teenager, I had left this town to "make it on my own". Now I was returning with a wife and child, and precious few dollars in my pocket.

It was mid-morning when we stepped down on the platform. It took only a quick glance to tell me that nothing had changed. There on the corner stood the hotel, the biggest building in town, and across the street from it the same sign announcing "Café" still hung. It was no warmer; the very air seemed to crackle. No one was there to meet us; the erratic crossing of the Pacific had disrupted our schedule and we had not bothered trying to inform anyone. In those days when few people had phones communication was not as simple as it is today.

One blast of its whistle and the train was on its way. But, thanks to good old efficient CNR, there on the platform stood our battered steamer trunk and our special wicker baby carriage, of which we were so proud. There also stood a solitary figure who was looking at us with some interest, and certainly we must have presented an unusual sight.

As we got closer I was able to recognize him as a farmer from south of town whose team I had looked after many times at the livery barn. He recognized me as well, and took in the situation immediately.

"I guess you want to get to your folks' place," he said. "You know your folks don't live here in town any more."

I knew that my parents had moved but was not sure where their new house was located.

"Come on. I'll take you out there," he said. And soon we, and our things were in his sleigh-box. What Clara's thoughts were one can only imagine. Ole Johnson used "snoose" copiously and, as always, the brown streaks on his chin attested to that fact. His horses stood dejected, heads down, and she could not have missed the long icicles that hung from their nostrils. Clara had never read Al Capp's L'il Abner. If she had she might well have thought that Lower Slobovia actually existed, and that somehow we had landed there.

It took only a few minutes before we pulled up into a farmyard on the outskirts of town. Soon we were greeted by exclamations of surprise, tears, the aroma of baking bread and a big cook-stove belting out heat - home.

A pleasant couple of weeks passed. It was a time of becoming reacquainted. It was Allan's time for paradise as he became thoroughly spoiled by his adoring grandparents. For Clara, it was a time to become accustomed to the prairie way of "freeze-drying" her wash. Every day she braved the cold to hang diapers on the line and bring them in later frozen stiff. I had two sisters within horse-and-sleigh range and my wife, who had thirteen siblings, soon found that she was part of another large, extended family. My young nieces soon attached themselves to this exotic creature from the south seas who "talked funny".

As for the town where I had grown up, it had changed little over the years. The café, with its lonely Chinese proprietor, was still in the same spot, although a different Mr. Lee was in charge. Across from it stood the hotel, at three storeys the largest building in town. There, from the age of twelve, I had a seven-day-a-week job which entailed tending to the hotel cow and milking her morning and night. I would also haul in enough water from the town pump to suffice for the day and throw into the basement as much wood as was needed to keep the furnace supplied. For this I was paid the sum of two dollars monthly, which I promptly turned over to my father.

One notable change was that the streets of town now had names, something that was not considered necessary before. We all knew where everybody lived. The street where we used to live was now called Clarence Street. Other people now lived in our house, and, half a block away was the wide gap where the huge livery stable, which was our business, used to stand. While I was away it was

| No Ordinary Job

destroyed in a spectacular conflagration that is talked about to this day.

But this idleness could not go on for too long. Our supply of dollars had dwindled down to a precious few, and it was time to get to work. I had not thought about what kind of work I might find in the middle of a prairie winter, and I was prepared to accept just about anything. My plan for the near future was to get enough money together so we could get back to the coast, where, if nothing else turned up, there was always the sea.

Chapter 2

Someone Who Had No Choice

The cold snap had broken and it was a bearable twenty below when, wearing my father's mackinaw, I planted myself on the highway to hitchhike to Saskatoon. This was Saskatchewan where nobody passed you by and within minutes a local farmer with business in the "city" had me in his pickup. He not only took me all the way to Saskatoon, but also went out of his way to drop me off at the employment office and picked me up too. A receptionist took my name and told me to wait for my name to be called. There were a good number of people ahead of me and more than an hour passed before I found myself seated before a counselor who wasted no time putting me in the picture.

"There's no work here," he informed me. "All the people you see in here are trying to get unemployment insurance. "But," he went on, "you don't qualify for unemployment. You've been out of the country, and you don't have the stamps. There's nothing I can do for you."

He must have sensed my disappointment, for he spent a few minutes chatting about New Zealand and my situation. "Anyway," he said finally, "you're in the wrong office. Radisson comes under North Battleford. Go see them there, maybe they'll have something for you."

So, the next morning, I boarded the bus in the other direction. I knew nothing about North Battleford, although I must have passed through it before. It was a small city and the employment office was only a short walk from the bus depot. Within minutes I was seated before a counsellor who gave me the same information I had received in

No Ordinary Job

Saskatoon – no work, not eligible for unemployment insurance. I was on my way out, when he called me back, "I do have something here but I don't know whether it will suit you - student nurse at the Saskatchewan Hospital. You know what that is, don't you? It's the mental hospital." Perhaps it was destiny but at that moment I had no idea how the wards of the Saskatchewan Hospital would change my life.

He seemed surprised when I said I'd take it. He didn't realize that he was dealing with someone who had no choice.

"Well, you don't have the job yet," he cautioned. "You have to go out there and be interviewed."

A short phone call and he turned to me again to inform me that I could have an interview that very afternoon.

"You know," he said, "this could be just the thing for you. It doesn't pay much to start, just one hundred and forty a month, but you get a raise and three weeks holiday every year. When you get there, you will be seeing a man named McLennan."

"How do I get there?" I wanted to know.

"It's out of town," he replied. "You'll have to take a taxi."

So there was no option but to dig into our dwindling supply of dollars. It turned out to be quite a distance.

"Visiting someone out there?" asked the driver.

When he heard I was to be interviewed for a job he told me that he used to have a girlfriend who worked there for a while and she thought it was a pretty good job.

The entrance was imposing – a wide flight of stairs led to double doors of an impressive width. These led into a long corridor that terminated at an information desk and switchboard. It seemed deserted. A well-dressed, elderly man sat smoking in one of the several chairs placed against the wall.

"She'll be back in a minute," he advised. "Just wait here." And sure enough, within minutes a friendly smiling woman came to take her place at the switchboard. It seemed Mr. McLennan could see me immediately and I was directed to his office on the second floor.

He turned out to be a thin, serious individual who appeared to be in his late thirties. He took from me the usual information, completed some forms and informed me that I would work on the wards until classes started in September. It was a Friday and I agreed to start on the following Monday, February 18, 1952. I promised to provide proof of completing Grade 11 as soon as I could get it. Fortunately, no one ever asked for it again.

In answer to questioning looks when I got home I announced that I had a job, and what it would be. The news did not elicit any great enthusiasm. People knew of the existence of the Saskatchewan Hospital, North Battleford, but never by that name. If spoken about at all, it would simply be referred to as "Battleford", a fearsome place of mystery and foreboding. We had Russian friends, and it was rumoured they had a son in "Battleford". (It was more than a rumour, I was to know him later). Certainly, in our town, we knew of no one who had been taken there and returned. In the early years of the war a family friend, Mr. Cobman, had worked there for a short time and during a visit, from which we children were excluded, there was a long whispered conversation punctuated by exclamations of astonishment and disbelief. And then there was John Kileen.

No Ordinary Job

When my family left the farm to move "to town" in 1939 the livery business my father had purchased included a house on a large lot. In one corner of the lot stood a one-room shack occupied by an old bachelor, John Kileen. People in those days were relaxed about such matters, and we didn't begrudge him the small amount of ground his shack and outhouse occupied. We simply planted our garden around them.

As far as we could tell, Mr. Kileen never left his place. He had a little dog for company and the small Roman Catholic community looked after his needs with periodic deliveries of groceries and wood. Unavoidably, given the circumstances, my mother started cooking a bit extra, and it became almost routine that something would be sent over to him - perhaps a pot of soup, or a meal that we were having. As for me, somehow it became my duty to be at his service – to keep his woodbox filled, clean up his shack, even do his dishes. There was no expectation of payment, although he once gave me a big copper penny of which there were still a few circulating at that time. Too polite to just walk away, I would sit for hours listening to him fulminate about Irish schools and bosses he had had. He didn't have a good word for anyone or anything, but he was never profane in my presence.

One day I reported as usual to find him in a strange position. His chair was leaned back against the wall, his head lolled to one side. Rushing home I cried out "He's dead!" My mother went to check and she was not long.

"He's not dead, he's just sleeping, but don't go there today."

And for a while he seemed to be his usual self. Then one day I overheard my mother say to my father that she had seen someone coming to Kileen's place. The person she named was well known to us as a producer of "homebrew". The very next day I appeared at his door to be greeted by a shocking sight. Axe in hand, he seemed to be in the process of destroying everything in his shack and then he came at me with weapon raised. Terrified, I ran for home and, this time, my mother took action.

"I'm going to tell Doctor Daly what happened," she said, going out the door. Doc Daly, the dentist - fellow Irishman, was one of the people concerned with the old fellow's welfare. The next day, through the window, I saw John Kileen for the last time. Walking with a cane, wearing a hat and a black suit I had never seen before, he followed an RCMP officer down the path to the street.

"They're taking him to Battleford," mother said. "He'll be better off there." Years later I found his name in the Death Book and saw that he had lived for only a year after admission.

So, for a couple of days, the mood around the house was somber. It was not only anxiety about what my job would entail, there was also the fact that I would be leaving my wife and child behind until I got a paycheque and found a place for us to live. Once again we reassured ourselves that this would be a stop-gap measure to carry us through until we got enough money together to look for another job, or return to New Zealand. In the interim, I would be living in the H hut – a residence for unmarried male staff.

Chapter 3

Giving a Hand

There was no reason to be displeased with H Hut. Compared to crews' quarters on a ship, or our bed-sitter in New Zealand, it was positively luxurious. A large common-room was furnished with sofas and comfortable chairs. There was a console model radio-phonograph; there was even a piano. The small, but adequate, rooms did not need to be shared. Even our morals were protected; a house-mother was there to make certain that we behaved properly, and that no females gained admission. Later I had my first meal in the staff dining room and found it was very good value for the half dollar it cost me.

My life experiences to that point had given me confidence that I could handle pretty well anything that might be thrown at me. Still, I was somewhat nervous at the prospect of my first day at this new job; I had absolutely no idea what to expect. Fortunately, a couple of staff from H hut volunteered to "show me the ropes". First, a good breakfast, then, it being a few minutes before seven, it was time to get a set of keys. In one corner of the basement there was a counter behind which stood the "keyman". He put my name in his book and gave me a set of keys from a numbered hook in the cupboard behind him. That number would be part of my identity from that day on. Shift change would be a busy scene with some staff picking keys up, others turning them in, but the keyman never forgot your number - where your keys belonged.

Then I set off to find the office of the Chief Attendant where I had been told to report. There, behind a desk, sat a stern looking man probably in his forties. Two other men dressed in suits stood at his desk. They were all looking at me inquisitively and I felt I had to say something.

"I'm starting work today and I was told to report here."

"What's your name?"

I told him and he had me repeat it.

"Where are you from?"

"New Zealand."

They exchanged looks, then, "Do you plan to stay in Canada?"

I explained that I actually was Canadian and that I planned to stay in the country. Without me being aware of it, my years in New Zealand had given me a bit of an accent which, no doubt, explained his questions.

The Chief Attendant studied me for a few seconds. Perhaps he was thinking "this fella's just about as tall as I am." Then he was brusque. "Go through that door and report to Mr. Edwards."

In time I was to learn that I had been talking to the redoubtable Charlie Batchelor whose very name seemed to strike fear into even the war veterans on the staff. As for me, I never had occasion to speak to the man again. On reflection one must accept that he must have possessed special qualities to develop his aura of assertiveness and command. He had come up "through the ranks" but it was hard to believe that at one time he was like the rest of us – changing beds and cleaning up the incontinent. Now he radiated authority. Perhaps he even had the power to shape events for a few years later he beat odds of millions to one to win the Irish Sweepstakes which was sold world-wide.

No Ordinary Job

When I passed through the doors I expected to find a hospital atmosphere with wards filled with bed patients. Instead I found a large dayroom where men of various ages dressed identically in work shirts and blue jeans moved about. Others sat in chairs lined against the walls. Behind the glass of a sort of cubicle I saw a man wearing a dress shirt and tie. I assumed he was in charge and such turned out to be the case. Wally Edwards' greeting could not have been more casual. After learning my first name he said, "Just wait around out there, in a few minutes they'll be going down for breakfast. And, oh yeah, put on one of those white jackets in that side-room." There were several hanging on hooks and I found one that fit well enough.

In time I would learn that 2A was the admission ward and that Wally Edwards was the supervisor. He was one of many whom I came to respect and admire. His calmness and unflappability made him the perfect choice to deal with frightened and confused new admissions.

Soon the call came, "Let's go boys!" and the patients began to stream out a side door and down the stairs. A "white-coat" counted them out as they filed by. It was then I noticed that several patients, all wearing grey bath robes, stayed behind.

We emerged into a cavernous section of the basement where our group joined a line filing past a serving counter manned by patients. To my eye it seemed there were hundreds of men in the huge dining area but our patients were accustomed to finding the area assigned to them.

The breakfast was simple. There was cooked cereal, already mixed with milk and sugar, and there were trays of buttered toast constantly being replenished. Some patients took several slices of toast and, having already sampled the excellent bread the hospital provided, I could understand why it was so popular. Patients carrying large enamel jugs of coffee, again already mixed with milk and sugar, circulated among the tables. The dishes were plastic and the only utensils provided were spoons.

We returned to a busy scene in the ward. Beds were being moved about and a padded table set up. "It's for shock," I was informed by one of the staff. Soon the doctor arrived wheeling in a small table holding what had to be the shock machine and, without delay, the first patient was ushered in and positioned on the shock table. My orientation was brief, "Hold him like this," and I was shown: elbow on the shoulder, hand grasping the arm and the other hand pressing down on the leg. It went very quickly – a gag was placed in the patient's mouth, the electrodes were applied to the patient's head and the doctor pushed the button. The result was dramatic, and something for which I was not prepared: first a shout, then a short period of rigidity, followed by violent convulsions. When these ceased the patient was turned on his side and we waited for him to take his first stertorous breath. He was then wheeled away to recover in another room. Surprisingly, there was little resistance. Occasionally, in a gesture of defiance, a patient would refuse to open his mouth for the gag, but this did not present any real problem. The gag was simply inserted when the patient's mouth flew open for the shout.

In short order the list was completed. The doctor left taking his shock machine with him. By this time the patients were beginning to regain consciousness and, as soon as they were steady, they were taken for a shower. When all were dressed they were taken downstairs for the breakfast they had missed. Maybe it was just a sense of relief, maybe it was a result of the treatment but there was an air of cheerfulness about the group. They were rewarded with a special breakfast – cooked or dry cereal, jam for their toast, coffee as they liked it.

No Ordinary Job

The rest of the morning passed uneventfully. Patients walked about, read, played cards. Some were called for interviews with doctors or psychologists. Staff took turns for a lunch break; most had brought their own lunch and did not patronize the staff cafeteria. Before going to the cafeteria I helped escort our patients to their lunch, which that day happened to be macaroni and cheese, salad, and cake for dessert. The staff cafeteria was serving the same.

I returned to the ward to find Wally Edwards waiting for me. "Good, you're back. You can go with Mr. Franklin and give him a hand downstairs." And he indicated a short, grey-haired man who greeted me with a wide smile. I was a bit taken aback when he led me through a door marked "morgue" and I could never have imagined what "giving a hand" would entail. There on the gurney lay the naked body of a woman completely cut open. I had seen dead persons before. In a Northern Ontario bush camp I had seen the body of a Finnish logger who had died from the kick of a horse. In Australia I had looked upon the body of a shipmate who, while intoxicated, had tried to swim ashore from our anchored ship and did not make it. Even so, I was unprepared for what I saw. If one could ignore the gaping opening in her body the woman seemed peaceful, at rest. She must have been a rather tall, strong woman, she had muscular arms and legs and, though her hair was greying, she did not appear aged.

"We have to sew her up," announced Mr. Franklin and, under his direction, we got to work using butcher's cord, curved needles and forceps. "Women are harder to do than men," he commented. "It's the fat."

I would have thought the fat would make it easier but I was in no position to express an opinion. Even though the stitching was done without much concern for neatness and spacing it was quite a lengthy process. At the end we covered our work with a shroud and transferred the lady to one of the drawers in the cooler.

By this time my first day was over and I had a great deal to think about as I made my way back to H hut. Sadly there was no one there to greet me with a "How was your day?"

Chapter 4

Lifelong Friends

It was the practice to start new staff on 2A until they got the feel of the place and developed a bit of confidence. Then they were transferred to other wards to gain experience in a variety of situations.

It was during my first week there, while I was still on 2A that an event occurred that haunts me to this day. My memories of how it developed are crystal clear and in my mind's eye I can see it unfolding as though it were yesterday.

In the early afternoon, just after lunch, Wally Edwards called the staff together. "The RCMP are bringing a guy in, and they say he's really violent." As a precaution, he phoned 4A and 6A and asked to borrow a man from each ward to give whatever help might be necessary.

Not long after we could hear a great commotion, shouts of "Help!" and "Let me go!" The doors were opened and two mounties forced in a man with his hands cuffed behind his back. Wally Edwards was his usual calm self. "You'll be okay here," and to the policemen, "Take the handcuffs off and leave him with us." This seemed to calm the patient and he allowed himself to be taken to a side room where he changed into a hospital gown and lay down on one of the beds. But this respite was short. Within a few minutes he came out, charging through the ward pulling on doors and hammering on windows. "Let me out of here! What is this place?" I can see him before me now - a tall thin man, balding on top, in his forties. He was amazingly strong; it took several staff to drag him to a unit on 6A. There he was held down long enough to be injected with a powerful sedative. It had no effect. The doctor was called and he arrived carrying a portable shock machine. Once again several staff held him down while he was shocked right there on the floor of the unit. He recovered almost immediately and was given a second shock with increased voltage. It was the end of the shift and I was glad to be able to get away and leave the unpleasant duty to others.

Still, when I arrived on the ward the next day I immediately asked about Mr. Gunderson. The answer rendered me speechless. "He died." How could that be, I wondered. As new staff I did not feel I had the right to ask too many questions but over time we all learned the details of what had transpired.

The effect of the second shock was not much better that that of the first. The patient continued his noisy hyperactive behaviour, trying to break down the unit door with his body and bare hands. It was obvious that if this continued he would do himself harm; but what to do with him? At some point the doctor suggested that he be put in a cold pack; at least there he could not do himself any injury.

There were still a few staff members who knew how to apply a cold pack. Before shock, it was a frequently used treatment option. It consisted of wrapping the patient in many layers of overlapping cold wet sheets until the patient resembled a mummy. Soon the patient's body temperature warmed up the sheets and the patient would drift into a deep sleep. So, Mr. Gunderson was shocked again and during the few minutes that he was unconscious the cold pack was applied. The patient awoke to find that he could not move any of his limbs, but he continued to be vocal, and strained continuously against his bindings. The staff waited for the cold pack to have its effect and when the patient became quiet, it was assumed that that was what had happened. But something did not seem normal and it was realized that he was not breathing. He was quickly unwrapped, but it was not possible to revive him. He had fought and strained against his wrapping until his heart just gave out.

Of course I felt affected by this news. I had gripped his arm, held him to the floor with a knee to his back and now he was dead. And I felt also for his family. What a shock it must have been when they were told that he died in the hospital the same day he arrived. Could there be any explanation that would satisfy them? I doubt it, and it is quite likely that the family held the hospital responsible for his death and had bad feelings toward the institution.

We learned also that the cause of his apprehension and violent behaviour was that he was beset by religious delusions, believing that he was the returned Christ under attack by the devil.

Years later I read a book written by an American psychiatrist in which he described a patient he had treated who demonstrated symptoms almost identical to our Mr. Gunderson. In his case he was able to save his patient although it was a near thing. We were not so fortunate. The same psychiatrist gave a name to this extreme condition: agitated paranoia and this diagnosis has now been added to the psychiatric lexicon.

It was during my first weeks at SHNB that I became acquainted with three other recent hires who were to become lifelong friends. Bill had never forgotten any joke he might have been told, and was constantly making up new ones of his own. Gordon, whose blond hair and good looks attested to his Scandinavian roots had a good voice and was apt to break into song at any time. Maurice was of a scientific and mechanical bent, an innovative tinkerer. Not one of them had yet reached the age of majority (twenty-one at that time), yet all three were already married with children. Although I had a couple of years on them, I had also married young and had a son. We found that we shared a similar sense of humour with a penchant toward the absurd. Another factor that bound us together was our poverty, and the way we reacted to it. We all lived in conditions that would be considered primitive today; in dwellings that lacked heat, water and sewer. In spite of this we never became down-spirited or overly discouraged. For that, I credit our friendship. We drew strength from each other, and our similar personalities were reflected in our attitudes toward our work. Where some might say that we lacked seriousness, and were somewhat irreverent, I maintain that the way we were able to identify with our patients, and the closeness we developed with many of them was to their benefit.

Outside the hospital I met another man who was to play a huge role in my life, and also become a lifelong friend. John Chwelos came from a well-known North Battleford family. They had a scrap metal business combined with an upholstery shop, and had the reputation of being "as honest as the day is long". The few hours of work I would put in with them helped us to survive, and the fishing trips to the northern lakes brought a few hours of pleasure (and some food) to our difficult lives.

Chapter 5

The Watchfuls

After a week or two on 2A, it was almost invariable that new staff would be sent to 10B. Possibly the thinking was "If he can make it there, he can make it anywhere." Nothing could have prepared a person for the assault on the senses that took place as soon as one stepped through the door. There was a strong smell of feces and urine. There was a constant hum caused by the sixty or seventy patients laughing, shouting or babbling. Some patients leaped about chasing objects only they could see; others fought off unseen opponents. There were men curled up in fetal position, others repeated gestures of which only they knew the meaning. This was 10B, the chronic ward.

Any uninitiated person could not help but be taken aback when first introduced to 10B. But after the initial shock wore off I was struck by a sentiment that has not left me to this day: how mysterious mental illness is and how cruel. Forget what you see before you and try to visualize these men as they once were – someone's sons and brothers, who laughed and joked and played games, went to school and learned to read. Maybe they tilled the soil, owned livestock, wrested a living from the begrudging Saskatchewan earth. And then something happened and whatever they had been, they were that no more. They were someone else or they were nobody. They were gone – as good as dead. They were no longer of this world.

One day I went through the records and found that, with rare exceptions, these patients had not had a visitor in years. And why should one expect different? Not long before these men were living naked and besoiled, on a par with beasts, what purpose could a visit have? To a loving parent or sibling it would be torture. No, better to let him go, forget him, he was gone.

I learned that 10B was fairly recently created and an improvement over past practices. Almost all of these patients had been brought over from another building, from a "chronic" ward where they had been locked away for years, even decades. There they had lived in unbelievable conditions, naked, incontinent. At night they slept on straw pallets in a heated ward. At intervals during the night it was the duty of staff to rouse the sleeping patients and herd them into the toilets. Even so, each morning there would be a good number of soiled or soaked pallets. These would be emptied, washed and refilled with straw. Of course these unfortunates never left the ward.

The story goes that the minister of health had become aware of conditions on the chronic ward and insisted on being taken there. He was horrified by what he saw for, really, this was a twentieth-century Bedlam. Directives came quick and fast. The patients were to be clothed. When it was objected that they would simply remove or destroy their clothing, the answer was to simply redress them. Secondly, the patients were to sleep in beds, and these were acquired. To make these patients more amenable to these changes in their lives it was decided to treat them, and most received a number of shocks. The expectations for success could not have been great yet the changes were striking. The patients were clothed, although most had a disheveled appearance. A few remained incontinent; those were toileted frequently and their mattresses protected by a rubber sheet. They now went downstairs for meals, and found their assigned area. A very few still needed help with their meals.

One of these was Doc Matthews, a pet to us all. A gentle old fellow, he could usually be found gazing out the window counting something off on his fingers. If you asked him what he was counting he would explain that it was the "watchfuls", little creatures that often gathered along the eaves and on window sills. There were red watchfuls and green watchfuls, each variety responsible for tasks that were beneficial to mankind. It was at mealtimes that the watchfuls gave Doc a special kind of difficulty. Every time he brought his spoon toward his mouth one or two, or a few, would persist in jumping on his spoon and he would have to brush them off before he could get any food into his mouth. The problem was that he could never get rid of them completely, which made it impossible for him to get any nourishment. He also refused to be fed since this did not solve the problem of the persistent watchfuls. The solution was to have staff posted behind Doc and just as he opened his mouth the staff would nudge his elbow and the contents of his spoon would end up in his mouth. Tears would flow, for Doc was a kind man who hated to swallow the friendly watchfuls but, in the end, he got sufficient nourishment in this fashion.

Doc had a beautiful blond daughter who came to visit him every summer. She drove up from California in a big Cadillac. Her visit was always a sort of occasion, a subject of conversation among staff.

"Doc's daughter came to visit him yesterday."

"Oh hell, I'm sorry I missed that."

She always left behind a box of goodies for Doc, the most important being many plugs of chewing tobacco of various brands. Likely she made a point of buying a few plugs every time she spotted a new brand. In fact Doc was often dissatisfied with her choices; he preferred the generic brand issued by the hospital. Curiously, the watchfuls did not interfere when he used tobacco and he was able to take bites out of his plug without hindrance. Perhaps they were repelled by the smell of the weed.

On a hot summer day, my day off, I decided to stop at the Dominion Café with my wife and son for a dish of ice cream – something we did frequently. As soon as we entered I could feel that something was not right. There was a strange stillness, although the restaurant was full, and everyone was looking in the same direction. There sat Doc and his daughter. The poor woman was red-faced, on the verge of tears. Doc was holding his fork toward his open mouth, brushing off the watchfuls in his characteristic way.

"Eat it, dad. It's good," she implored.

I walked over to their table and whispered to her, "I'll take him outside."

"C'mon Doc. Let's go out."

"Sure, son."

The daughter joined us soon after, having stopped to pay the bill.

"I thought he would like to get out for a change," she said. "Why does he do that?"

I didn't try to explain the watchfuls to her. "It's just something he does. We have to feed him."

I did not see the lady again, although she continued her yearly visits.

Because of his eccentricity, Doc took his meals in a small side room off the dining area along with a few others who had eating problems. Some just needed to be fed, others bolted their food so rapidly that they represented a choking danger. In this same room one of my favourite characters. Louis Zokal, took his meals. Although he seldom spoke, I had soon realized that, psychotic as he no doubt was, he was also a mischievous trickster. Somehow, he had come into possession of a new-looking denim smock, of the type that Saskatchewan farmers wore for trips to the city, or other dress-up occasions such as Massey-Harris movie night. He managed to retain it through all the years I was there. Always on the move, he would often be seen carrying a broom with which he would sweep up some corner of the ward. After making a neat little pile he would somehow manage to snatch it up with one swipe of his hand. This he would deposit into his smock pocket for future use. He had his reasons.

Louis had developed the sport of "playing with one's food" to a fine art. Everything he was served: stew, dessert, drink he would mix together in a disgusting mess from which he would take the occasional spoonful. But he really came into his own when he noticed a new staff assigned to the room. Then his hand would go to his pocket and a handful of rubbish would be flung into his bowl and mixed into a stomach-churning concoction. Louis would take a spoonful from his bowl and, at a moment when the new staff's attention was on some other patient, he would flip it on the floor, then hold the filthy spoon near his mouth while pretending to chew. While the unsuspecting staff slowly turned green, Louis would glance in my direction, his eyes sparkling with mischievous good humour. He knew I was on to him and that he could trust me to go along with his harmless pranks. Since he wasted so much of his food he was rail-thin and, in hindsight, perhaps we should have been more conscientious where his nourishment was concerned. But then again, perhaps it was to his advantage, for he lived to a great old age. More than a quarter century later I returned for a Saskatchewan Hospital reunion to find him still alive, in his late eighties and still ambulant. He seemed to recognize me; I thought he gave me a wink. Maybe I just imagined it.

One of my friends, and co-worker, Maurice told me an amusing story about Louis. Louis slept with a couple of other patients in a sort of verandah that used to be part of the TB ward. One winter night there was a very strong wind blowing and it was not possible to get the area heated sufficiently for comfort. The staff were busy providing extra covers, and as Maurice spread an extra blanket over Louis' thin frame, the latter came out with one of his rare utterances. "Good night for stealing wood."

Chapter 6

Built To Last

When construction began on SHNB at the beginning of the last century, it must have been one of the largest construction projects in the new province. For an almost totally agrarian society, with a population of less than half a million, it had to be a significant financial drain. Nevertheless, even today, one can see that it was built to last. The thick brick and stone walls, the high ceilings and wide corridors put to shame many institutions built more recently. The frequently spaced, ten-foot high windows were not barred as may be seen in psychiatric hospitals in other provinces and in American states.

The impressive front entrance opens into a wide hall bordered by offices, and ends in a reception area. To the left and right locked doors open to the patient wards, even numbered on the male side, odd numbered on the female side. There are five wards on each side on each level. Thus 2A to 10A (1A to 9A on the female side) are on the first level. As one would presume, the same arrangement with the designation B, exists on the second level. Jutting above 10B there is another ward, now designated 10C. Originally intended to accommodate unmarried male staff, it later became simply another ward with room for sixty patients.

Below this massive structure was excavated a huge basement which was put to good use. Apart from the patients' dining areas, already mentioned, it contained the kitchen and bakery, the pharmacy, the dentist office, the library, and, of course, the morgue. Here also were found the occupational therapy department, the sewing room, the ever-busy barber shop and beauty salon. The hydrotherapy areas remain, although they are no longer in use.

In separate buildings were found other shops and essential facilities: the tailors and dry-cleaners, the upholstery shop, garages and other repair shops.

The power-house, whose tall chimney dominated the countryside, never failed to provide all the light, heat and hot water required. Attached to it, which seems fitting since it used so much of its product, was the laundry, indubitably the busiest workshop of all.

And it wasn't all work. The main building had a large auditorium, where films were shown, and dances held. For the use of patients and staff there was a skating ring and a two-sheet curling rink. For summer recreation there were tennis courts and ball diamonds as well as an eighteen-hole golf course, which attracted golfers from near and far. There were no green fees; one could simply tee-off any time and enjoy the day. Should there be a lost ball, there was always no end of willing searchers.

Over the years a number of cottages and a three-storey apartment building were provided for the use of essential personnel and other staff. Until the 1950's there was an elementary school to serve the children of staff who lived in the grounds. All in all, it was a desirable place to live and raise a family.

And the whole complex, placed as it was on high ground overlooking the valley of the North Saskatchewan river, presents one of the more beautiful vistas of flat-land Saskatchewan. And this vista was also enjoyed by patients as I was to discover.

One day a visitor came to see a patient named Fred and I was sent to the 12 building to find him. He was one of the members of the "barn gang" who did the milking morning and evenings. "Where can I find him?" I wanted to know.

| No Ordinary Job

"Well he's probably at his place down by the river," a staff member said as he gave me directions. "You can take your car if you want."

Parking the car on the shoulder I followed the path he described. I came upon a surprising sight. There was a line of huts made out of old lumber, pieces of tin and old windows. I saw old fellows sitting in discarded armchairs, cats sleeping on their laps and on the slope of the hill well laid-out vegetable gardens. Fred was there in front of his hut, a pipe in his mouth, an orange cat on his lap. He came along with me to see his visitor although he did not seem too enthusiastic about it. When I complimented him about the gardens he said, "Well, the river's right there, we've got lots of water, and it's good soil." I found that these old patients would bring their produce in to sell on "visitors day" when people would come up from the city to buy vegetables and tour the grounds. I found that few of the newer employees were aware of this community, only old-time staff.

Chapter 7

Money Well Spent

Even though it was a comfortable life living in H hut I found myself missing my wife and son terribly. A friend, John Chwelos, put me in touch with a man who would rent us the ground floor of his house. It was off sewer and water, but it had a cookstove and there was a big woodpile where we could help ourselves. Best of all, the rent was only $25 per month. John supplied us with a bed and mattress, which I would pay off over time by working for him. By the time all of this was negotiated the last of our money was gone, but I expected to be paid in a few days when I would have put in a month's work.

So it was that my brother-in-law brought Clara and Allan out to North Battleford on a day in mid-March. With them came a veritable treasure trove: sheets, pillows, blankets, all we needed in that line. And, best of all, boxes and boxes of my mother's canning. There were pickles and jams, beef and chicken, home-canned pork and beans, and many jars of Saskatoon berries, the memory of which makes my mouth water to this day. A big bag of potatoes came as well, and also pots and pans to cook them in. We still had a box of Ancora, the New Zealand infant formula and that, supplanted by milk, had Allan looked after. I had a bus pass that would get me to work. All in all we felt well equipped to get through the first few days until my pay cheque arrived.

The days went by and the anticipated cheque did not materialize. Then we were faced with a crisis. Our boy, now a six-month-old, was usually the epitome of the "good" baby. He seldom cried and, as a rule, slept soundly through the night. But then, one evening, he began to "grizzle" as

No Ordinary Job

New Zealanders say, whimpering, crying and fretting. He would fall asleep for a few minutes, then awake with a sharp cry that we hadn't heard before. It was obvious he was in pain and Clara surmised that he might be teething. Finally, in desperation, we crushed half an aspirin in some of my mother's jam and succeeded in having him swallow the mixture. He eventually fell into a fitful sleep, probably from pure exhaustion. Morning came after a practically sleepless night. I had to go to work. Of course we had no phone so all I could do during the day was worry and hope to find things improved when I got home. But what I found was a wife in tears and a child who was, even to the untrained eye, very sick. Naturally, I broke down as well, and there we were, the three of us, sobbing away. I remember that in my fear and frustration I blurted out "Why did we come back to this bloody country?" Then I declared, "I'm going to get a doctor." But medicare was still years in the future. The hospital had an excellent medical plan for its employees, but one needed to have worked there for three months to qualify and I was two months short of that. And we were penniless.

The place where we were living was on the very outskirts; beyond us was an empty snow-covered expanse. So it was some distance to the city centre. As I walked along the icy streets I rehearsed in my mind the story I would tell the doctor when I found one; how we had recently arrived from New Zealand, how my cheque had been delayed and that I would certainly pay him as soon as I had some money. It was, without a doubt, the low point of my life; never had I felt so discouraged and helpless. But soon I would meet a man who would lift my spirits and restore my hope.

It was already dusk and near the end of the business day when I turned into the first door with a doctor sign. The waiting room was empty except for a man dressed in a hat and overcoat. There was a receptionist behind the counter and I addressed myself to her, "My boy is very sick and I need a doctor." At this point the gentleman spoke, "My name is Doctor Serimgeur. Tell me what's wrong with your boy." I went into my rehearsed appeal, on the verge of breaking down again. He cut me short, "Let's go have a look your boy." I followed him to his car then directed him to our home. On the way, he quizzed me a bit about our move from New Zealand. He had a strong Scottish burr and it is possible that his kind treatment of us was affected by the fact that he was a recent arrival in Canada.

He would have noted the Spartan conditions under which we were living. At that point we did not even have a table. But he must also have noticed that it was clean and orderly, and that the baby was well cared for.

He likely suspected where the trouble lay, for he went straight to an examination of Allan's ears.

"He has a bad ear infection," he said. "He must be in terrible pain."

"He needs penicillin," he went on. "I'll give you a prescription. Fill it right away and start the treatment."

It was time to demean myself again. "Doctor," I said, "for the first time in my life I have no money at all. I need to find a pharmacy that will give me credit."

He considered for just a moment. "It's better if I get it and add it to your account."

When he emerged from the pharmacy he handed me a small package. "There's some penicillin syrup. Just follow directions. There's also some children's aspirin. Give him a double dose to start."

As he drove me home all I could do was repeat, "I can't thank you enough. When I get my cheque I'll pay you right away." To which he responded, "that'll be fine."

We were concerned that Allan would refuse the medication but it was as though he knew it was for his benefit. He swallowed the mixture of banana-flavoured penicillin and crushed aspirin without objection, and not long after fell into a merciful sleep. During the night he awoke, took some nourishment and another dose, and when I left for work in the morning both mother and child were in a deep sleep. That afternoon when I got home I found a happy, smiling boy, his old self. He finished the bottle of antibiotic and has never had so much as an earache since.

Having already lowered myself to beg, it was easier to do it a second time. Not far from us a new grocery store had opened, the Corner Market. When I entered there were no customers and I was able to tell my story to the proprietor without that extra embarrassment. I asked for credit for bread and milk. She reflected for a time, then told me I could have credit to a maximum of twenty dollars. As it happened that was more than enough. As for that other essential of life for New Zealanders, tea, I confess to filching a few spoonfuls from the hospital kitchen.

The day came when I finally got paid and, since it was for a month and a half, we felt quite flush. Actually, it was barely a living wage but we learned to stretch it out. What I remember is the great satisfaction I felt when I was able to settle my debts. At the doctor's office the receptionist could find no bill and had to call Doctor Serimgeur out. I welcomed the opportunity to express once again my gratitude for his kindness and, in response to his questions, assured him that Allan was completely cured. He conferred with the receptionist for a few minutes and she presented me with a bill for twenty dollars, which I was happy to pay. It was money well spent.

Certainly, Dr. Serimgeur would have been our family doctor but that was not to be. Shortly after we learned he was no longer in North Battleford; there was some suggestion that he had moved to California. Wherever it might have been I hope he had a successful and rewarding life. My gratitude for his kindness and humanity is as strong today as it was more that half a century ago.

As for the Corner Market, it became a flourishing business. Within the year it had expanded and became a sort of mini-supermarket, and we became loyal customers. The proprietors were an unusual couple. The wife was tiny, almost skeletal, she would never make 100 pounds on the scale. The husband, on the other hand was a large, silent, brooding man who usually let his wife deal with the customers. To look at them one would not have credited them with great business acumen, yet their store was very successful. Twenty-five years later it was still flourishing with new owners.

From this point in our lives things could only improve. Soon it would be summer. We were now covered by the medical plan. The hospital credit union was there for emergencies. We were able to move to a little apartment with heat and water. It was still a hand-to-mouth existence but now, at least, there was something in the hand.

Chapter 8

Remember This

The harsh winter of 1951-52 finally came to an end. An early spring was followed by a truly glorious summer. My probationary period was over, and our family was covered by the medical plan; no more worries in that regard. I was also outfitted with two pairs of trousers, produced in the hospital's own tailor shop. The hospital also had its own dry-cleaners, where we could have our trousers cleaned periodically. The sum of it all was that life took on a brighter hue.

It also turned out to be a bumper year for Saskatoon berries. People could not remember a time when this beautiful prairie berry was as plentiful or as luscious. With our Allan in his wicker carriage we roamed the river banks and returned with buckets brimming. Bread and butter, Saskatoons with cream; that was a complete meal for us and we had it often.

But the time was fast approaching when some decision had to be made. My plan originally was to find a way to get through the winter, put together enough money to get back to the coast and the sea, maybe even return to New Zealand with all its disillusionment. However, when it came time to decide what to do, we were faced with some hard facts. My miniscule salary did not allow for any savings; in fact, without the few dollars I was able to earn at Chwelos' upholstery business and scrapyard we could not have made it. We also had a small loan at the hospital credit union. In effect, the decision was made for us: we had to stay where we were, and make the best of it. I was hired as a student nurse, and that's what I would be.

Looking back, I can admit that the decision was made without much soul-searching or regret. The job was beginning to grow on me. Apart from the meager salary, about which nothing could be done (and there were people working for less), there were many advantages. There was nothing strenuous about it, and the work environment was comfortable. I seemed to get along well with the patients, and for many I had developed a real affection. With few exceptions I found my workmates to be admirable and superior people. As well, I had already come to feel that it was no ordinary job, that we were doing work that was special and essential and, perhaps, work that not everyone could do.

And so it was that on a day in September, 1952, I turned up with about half a hundred others, in the lecture room for registration and instructions. We could see that women outnumbered the men by about two to one and that most of the women were young, recent high school graduates. The men were more of a mixed group – there were young high school grads among them, but there were as many who, like myself, had worked in other fields. One of our number was in his fifties, a retired RCMP officer. This preponderance of women was to result in the posting of women to male wards, something that never took place in the opposite direction, at least during my time at SHNB.

On a table we could see stacks of hefty tomes and we were instructed to each take a copy. It was our syllabus, an outline of what we would be studying for the next three years. A quick glance through the pages was enough to make one realize that this was not going to be any cakewalk. There were sections on psychiatry and psychology, psychiatric and general nursing, anatomy and nutrition – serious business.

Psychiatry was taught by the doctors, and we thus came to know these individuals whom we saw almost daily about the wards, but who, to this point, had been only names to us.

They were an interesting group, the medical staff at SHNB. The majority were Polish, but Germany, Ireland and, of course, Canada were also represented. At the beginning there was only one woman among them, a tiny German woman. Dr. Demay, the superintendent, was a francophone, Saskatchewan born.

I can safely say that we all enjoyed the lectures of the medical personnel. It seemed to us that they enjoyed imparting their knowledge, and that they approached this extra duty with seriousness and dedication. Personal anecdotes and clinical demonstrations made their lectures interesting and stimulating, and we looked forward to them.

A class favourite was the colourful Dr. Ehrlich. He was related to the famous Dr. Paul Ehrlich, a Nobel Prize winner, who discovered the Salvarsan treatment for syphilis; with his wire-rimmed spectacles, bushy mustache and greying red hair he epitomized perfectly the popular conception of a German or Austrian psychiatrist. An animated and entertaining lecturer, he would exhort us to "remember this for the next two hundred years". His clinical demonstrations were pure theatre. He once put the causes of mental illness in a nutshell for us with the statement: "If it wasn't for sex and religion we'd all be out of a job."

Dr. Podilski, during the course of his life as a physician, must have been terribly affected by the tragic deaths of children by choking. He believed strongly that all nurses and parents should know how to perform an emergency tracheotomy, and he devoted one complete hour of his lecture time to showing us how it might be done. He finished by saying, "Now you know how to do it. I hope you won't stand by and watch someone die when you can save his life." As it happened we had two patients die choking on food, beyond help by the time a doctor arrived. In both cases it happened on the sick ward where scalpels were readily available. I often ask myself whether I would have had the nerve to attempt the procedure had I been there. Fortunately, I was never tested. Even so, many of us began to carry a sharp pocketknife, prepared to save any choking child we might come upon. As far as I know, none of us ever had this experience.

Apart from the fact that the course content was extensive and thorough, there were other factors that made continuing the course an even greater strain. In accordance with practices of the time students had to maintain their ward duties as well as their lessons. Those fortunate enough to be on day duty were entitled to be released from duty in order to attend lectures. Those on afternoons had to come in early, as many hours as was necessary. Night duty imposed great physical demands. Students had to wake up after a few short hours sleep, make their way to the lecture room, then return home to attempt to get in a couple more hours sleep before having to head out again. For those living on the grounds, this was not too onerous, but for those of us who were married with families, those living in town, it meant losing a couple of hours to bus travel. In my case, car ownership was something for the future. Our little paycheques did not permit us to think about such luxuries.

Fortunately it was hospital policy to rotate shifts so that night duty was one month out of three and this made it survivable. Even so, the end of the third year and graduation was a goal much looked forward to. Final exams, with their written and practical components were dreaded and the period of awaiting one's marks was an anxious one. Finally, it was over and time for the elaborately staged graduation ceremonies with the usual

No Ordinary Job

speeches, presentations and attendance by family members. Usually in the same night was the graduation ball – all the girls with their graduation gowns – and a chance to see all the doctors with their spouses – a night when the hospital went all out.

One last hurdle: those graduates who sought registration had to pass a final exam set by the University of Saskatchewan. Not all sat it; it was not obligatory. Those who passed it up could still practice and their duties were the same. The main differences were a pay differential – quite insignificant – and probably less opportunity for promotion.

So the majority settled down to what was, in most cases, a lifetime career. There were many advantages to doing so: a comfortable inside job, generous holidays, a good pension scheme and a medical plan totally covered by the province. Throw in the many recreational opportunities on the hospital baseball diamonds, curling rinks and golf course and it is easy to understand what made the career attractive.

After graduation, as expected in any hospital, we became the mainstay. The hospital functioned because we were there. We were depended on to know how to do what was necessary and, in fact, we did. We could draw blood and transfuse it; we could give oxygen by various means in post-op care. As well, there was our knowledge of how to care for and react to all kinds of psychiatric problems. For this, no doubt, experience was as valuable as "book learning".

When, twenty-five years later, I returned for a reunion, I found most of my classmates there; some retired, some approaching the end of their careers. What was surprising was the number of doctors who, after retirement, had also remained in the area. One would have thought they would seek warmer climes or a more cosmopolitan and exciting environment. Likely the relaxing rural atmosphere had something to do with it.

Chapter 9

Could More Have Been Done?

2A, 10B, 6A - that seemed to be the routine. 6A was termed the refractory ward, although the term was seldom used among the staff. The residents of the ward were supposed to be difficult to handle, although most of them were past that stage and the circumstances that had brought them to that ward were long forgotten. There were a couple of patients who had been "OIC'd", sent there by Order-in-Council of the courts for murder or other offences. But mostly it was a matter of convenience: since almost all were able-bodied they went to work on gangs every day, and could be more easily collected by confining them to one ward.

What did differentiate the ward was the presence of twelve single rooms, "units" we called them, which formed part of it. In each unit there was a single tiny window, high on the wall, out of reach. The door was double-sheathed, and in its centre was a peep-hole. New patients with a tendency to violence were brought there, as were patients from other wards who had gone "up the pole" and needed to be treated.

While not one of the units could qualify as the legendary "padded cell", measures were taken to prevent a patient from causing injury to self or others. On first being placed in a unit a patient would be stripped and two "strong sheets" were thrown into the unit with him. These were made of several layers of canvas, cross-stitched hundreds of times so that a patient had no hope of taking them apart. Patients would usually huddle in a corner making use of what they had. When, after a few shocks, it seemed that the patient had settled down he would get a mattress on the floor. The next step would be for a bed like everyone else.

Sometimes the progress of the patient would be misjudged. On a few occasions during my time there a patient had become disturbed, disassembled his bed, and used parts of the bed frame as weapons. Generally they would attack the door. The way to handle such a situation without injury to patient or staff was to make sure sufficient manpower was on hand. At an opportune moment the door would be flung open and the patient would be overwhelmed and rendered harmless. Then the poor fellow would go back to strong sheets and start over again.

The units had one permanent resident. This was John Sharp who, for reasons that I never determined, was deemed the most dangerous patient in the place. His appearance and manner could not be better designed to belie this assessment. Glinting blue eyes, glasses, white hair and beard made him appear the epitome of a kindly granddad.

At any rate John Sharp was kept permanently on 6A, in a unit that had been made quite livable for him. He had a comfortable chair and a table. He also had a wheelchair to get around on, since he had lost a leg. Somewhere he had a prosthesis which was denied him. So were clothes; he lived full-time in what we called a closed gown. No one could ever tell me what he had done to merit this distinction. The closest thing that I heard was. "He's a paranoiac." Later, in our lectures, we learned that paranoia was one of the rarest diagnoses in the psychiatric lexicon. Dr. Jedlicki tried to explain to us the differences between paranoid schizophrenic and paranoia. The schizophrenic believes that he is being persecuted and must find a reason why this is so. This could give rise to no end of delusions such as "I am Christ returned." The paranoiac remains in the world of reality and can usually find some logical or legitimate reason for his persecution. Having a real enemy makes it possible for him to retaliate and this renders him very dangerous.

I have to admit, when I was first posted to 6A on the afternoon shift I was quite won over by him. He gave me a friendly greeting and asked mannerly questions about my home and family. At the time he had it on his agenda to make a horse lead out of braided horsehair for the supervisor, Lou Gubbe. I agreed to obtain for him some necessities to complete the project. Among them a "three-inch, black, japanned harness snap, fifteen cents the world over." Whether he ever completed the lead I cannot say.

Most of his time was spent writing and he was provided with all the writing material he needed. He was quite productive. Often he would entrust a staff to deliver or mail one of his missives to the superintendent, or the police, or perhaps the Prime Minister. These letters of complaint, full of sarcasm or veiled threats, were always couched in fine English and totally devoid of profanity. Often the object of his ire was no longer on the ward or no longer employed at the hospital. These letters were added to his voluminous file and from them I learned that I, at first one of his favourites, was now denounced as a "spy" a "lackey" a prevaricator and a scoundrel.

But his literary efforts were not limited to these attempts to obtain justice for himself. His file bulged with samples of his poetry, which, rightly, should have been collected and published as a literary work of a special mind. For example, watching the "gangs" being rounded up in the mornings inspired him to become their champion:

Who are these creatures

So mute and so cowed

Surveying with dead eyes

The shuffling crowd

Herded by brutes all

Shouting abuse

In their ill-fitting clothes

From the caps to the shoes.

    A glance into the day-room as he wheeled by from the washroom moved him to pen this immortal couplet:

One blind up, one blind down,

Asshole wipers all around.

    He never missed a thing, and he had been around long enough to be familiar with all aspects of our work.

    But leave 6A and step through the door into 8B you would likely run into a man whose illness certainly gave him no pleasure, but instead was the source of perpetual suffering and pain. In its strangeness and perplexity his case was on a par with Oliver Sack's man who mistook his wife for a hat. Red haired, muscular Jim Whitehall would probably be over six feet tall if straightened out. But the person you would meet would be bent over to the point where his upper body was almost parallel to the floor. He would turn toward you a face twisted by agony and strain and explain the reason for his predicament.

    "Well, I've got this 600-pound woman on my back and she won't get off."

    And, if you demurred and ventured to explain that there was nothing on his back that you could see, he would not argue. He would simply give you a scornful look and move on. He knew she was there, and if you couldn't see her there was nothing he could do about that.

The posture he adopted - bent double at the waist, a bending of the knees as well, was one that is most uncomfortable. We tried it, and could not hold it for more than a few minutes, and to walk while maintaining that position required good effort.

8B had a mixed patient population. The majority would be considered extended care in today's vocabulary, but there were also a number of dayroom patients who were up and about; most of these were able to go downstairs for meals and, as an ambulant patient, Jim was one of them.

One day the supervisor Jimmy Chrysler saw him laboring up the stairs and took pity on him and added him to the list of those fed on the ward. At the table he had to turn his chair sideways in order to fit both himself and his invisible passenger on the seat.

Bedtime must have been a great relief for Jim. He could finally straighten out and take the weight off his legs. But even there he could not really be comfortable. He had to lie on his side on the very edge of his bed in order that his constant companion could have some room.

But he proved he could move with surprising speed. One day Frank Row gave him a playful boot in the rear, "Straighten up, Jim." He took off running but Jim caught him before he reached the end of the corridor. He then delivered a gentle reproach, "Don't do that again."

Whether his passenger fell off, or held on for dear life is something only he could know, but those who were present saw an amazing transformation before their eyes. His face began to regain its usual expression of strain, eyes bulging, teeth clenched while his back bowed to the weight as his burden assumed her usual position. "You should have seen it," marveled Frank. "It was uncanny, unbelievable, eerie."

It would be nice to report that eventually he received treatment that freed him from his delusion and allowed him to be boarded out along with the majority when this happened in the 70's and 80's. Unfortunately, this was not the case. His heart gave out under the strain. It might be stretching it to say that his burden was so real to him that it had the same effect as though it was really there. Still, it is not unreasonable to suspect that the unnatural posture he had to assume and the great amount of effort required from him to move about might well have affected his circulatory system. Could more have been done? Probably not.

Chapter 10

A Broken Reed

The patient in charge of 8A kitchen was Art Amos, a cantankerous old farmer from the Richard area. His conscientiousness and organizational skills probably made him a success on the farm until his mood swings and temper tantrums made him impossible to live with. His assistant was Ed Miller – a thin, almost emaciated man in his forties. His usual pose was to stand off to the side with his hands clasped in front of him, face pinched, lips compressed. While he knew the elements of his job, his lack of initiative motivated Art Amos to the limit.

The scenario was unchanging. "Set out the trays," would order the old farmer. He never addressed Ed by name. Ed would jump to the task, set out the required number of trays, then go back to his place and reassume his usual pose. The old farmer tried to be tolerant, "Come on, you know what to do. Put a cup and plate and spoon on each tray." Again Ed would jump to the task, complete it and return to his usual position.

"Now dish out the spuds," and so it would go on until, inevitably, Art would lose all patience, "You know what to do. Why do I have to tell you every time? Bloody idiot!"

What the old farmer didn't know was that the man he had just called an idiot possessed intelligence on a par with Einstein. He came from an academic family and had a fascinating and unusual history. He had been one of those child prodigies we hear about from time to time. He entered Harvard at the age of sixteen. There he specialized in linguistics, with a special interest in Icelandic sagas. As a scholar he distinguished himself and won a plethora of scholarships and awards. When he received his PHD, Harvard did not want to let him go, and he was offered a professorship in the linguistics faculty. He proved a failure at this and the University withheld tenure and released him. At a series of less illustrious colleges he did no better and even a high school position proved beyond him. The time came when he ended up in the parental home, unable to succeed at any employment. He became uncommunicative and slovenly, and eventually became one of our permanent residents.

I always had a lot of sympathy for him, and felt for him when he was ridiculed or insulted. Perhaps if a different path had been chosen for him he might have been saved. Someone at Harvard should have realized that this introverted and introspective man who lived to work within library walls delving into ancient times, would be totally lost standing before a class of cynical and challenging college students.

Dr. Ehrlich expressed similar views when he brought him to our class for a clinical demonstration. He attempted to engage him in an intellectual discussion but elicited from him answers completely lacking in emotion or imagination. After sending him away he was vivid in his explanation. "If you put this man on a desert island with a case of beans but no can opener, and a book of Icelandic sagas, he would lose himself in the sagas and starve to death. He would not think of smashing a can open with a rock so he could survive."

Naturally, he was on one of the "parole" wards; no one would consider him an escape risk. While his ward may have held as many as a hundred patients he was withdrawn from all of them. His diagnosis was simple schizophrenia, but he was the classic "broken reed". His efforts to excel, not so much to satisfy himself as to live up to the expectations of others, eventually overwhelmed him and he escaped into psychosis. Over the years I have come across more than one example of such tragedies. They may not be in institutions but, in spite of their intellectual superiority, they fail in life. Often on social assistance, or in a series of low-paying jobs, they never seem to measure up to their potential. Unable to form any meaningful relationship with another person they live, with rare exceptions, single and childless.

Ed Miller's tragic case presents a lesson that we can all take to heart. Like anything else on earth, a person can only be pushed so far, beyond that is the breaking point.

Chapter 11

Out In the World

One dark winter morning I reported to 6A just before seven for the morning dayshift. In a corner of the dayroom I noticed a patient on his hands and knees scrubbing the floor, something totally out of the usual.

"Who's this new guy?" I asked. I was informed that he had arrived as a transfer from Weyburn Hospital the day before.

"So, how come he's scrubbing the floor at this time of day?"

"He wanted to do it; wouldn't take no for an answer, so we just let him go ahead."

A few minutes later, it being almost time to go down for breakfast, I went over to tell him to put the cleaning stuff away. He turned up to me a smile of such beauty, so gentle and benevolent. His scalp was shaved bald, and one could not miss the recent lobotomy scars. I did not at that moment realize that this was the beginning of a genuine, if unusual friendship.

I found out that he had been confined in Weyburn since 1930 after having been found not guilty, by reason of insanity, of the murder of his brother-in-law. Recently, in Weyburn, he had for some reason killed another patient by beating him to death with what we called a hair broom. Following that he was lobotomized and transferred to SHNB. There, on 6A, his willingness to help, and his ingratiating manner soon won us over. He was put in charge of meals for patients in units, and the small room where the trays were assembled became in his mind, and

No Ordinary Job

we were quite happy to leave it so, his office, his domain. We had a Chinese patient, Toy, who had a little business going, shining shoes and rolling cigarettes for the staff. News began to circulate that Toy, who had also committed murder, was soon to be released on parole after being confined for twenty years. When this was borne out Paul inherited the business, although he claimed to have bought it. So the shoeshine kit and the cigarette roller became his property.

In fact, the business was quite lucrative, relatively speaking. A shoeshine was a quarter and many staff used this service. You could bring him a packet of tobacco and he would roll it into good-looking cigarettes for a quarter. The hospital issued cigarette tobacco, snoose and chewing tobacco practically on demand. Paul, as well as the majority of patients, did not smoke, but he drew his quota anyway and was probably given a few extra packets as well. So he was able to sell a good number of ready-mades to the staff for twenty-five cents. At the time I was trying to gain fluency in French and I provided him with the cigarette tubes, ostensibly in return for conversational practice. It actually turned out to be good value. He was a demanding teacher, "I told you this yesterday and you forgot it already?" he would remonstrate in his accented English.

This attitude and demeanor carried over into his ward duties. Although only of medium height he carried himself with an air of authority. Since his lobotomy he found it more practical to keep his head shorn. He had a pair of suspenders, something usually denied to patients, and a typical pose found him standing at his office door, thumbs hooked around his braces, looking in charge. Occasionally a patient might invest him with more authority than he actually possessed, and ask him for information or for a favour. With them he was terse, "We won't discuss that now, see Mr. Gubbe later."

The time came when he actually spoke to me about the crime that led to his lifelong confinement. At the time of its occurrence he was working as a sort of gardener handyman at a convent, where he had a room and took his meals. His sister, mother of eight children, lived in the area with her husband, Ambrose Briard.

"Something told me I had to kill him. I had a revolver. One day he was taking me back to town in the democrat. I sat on the back seat. I didn't want him to suffer or be afraid; he was such a nice man. I saw some crows in the sky so I said to him, 'Look at all the crows, Ambrose.' And when he looked I shot him. Now I'm sorry. He was such a nice man."

I did not encourage him to talk about it again, and now I wish I had because in my mind a question remains unanswered. How did he come to possess a handgun in those years?

When the time came that I was leaving the hospital to move to another province, I decided to try to take Paul out to my home for a visit. This was an iffy situation; OIC patients such as Paul were not, as a rule, allowed to leave the hospital. However, because of my long service and unblemished record, I got permission. We found him a decent looking sport coat from ward stock. On the drive to town he marveled over the traffic and the roads. Then abruptly, he said, "Stop and get some beer." This was totally unexpected and presented me with a quandary: do I just find some reason to refuse? Do I make him go into the hotel with me, which would mean I didn't trust him? In the end I decided to leave him in the car while I bought a six-pack from the beer parlour; and I was relieved to see him still there when I returned. At home, my wife was, understandably, a bit nervous. She had not been overly enthusiastic about the whole idea, but Paul soon put her at ease as he marveled at our simple home, our stove, our refrigerator. We had a full-length mirror on our bathroom door and he spent some time examining himself before it. It was then that I realized that there were no mirrors on the wards. Patients could never see themselves. One wonders what effect this depersonalization had on recovery.

I opened a beer for him and as he raised it to his lips he said, "This is the first beer for me since April third, 1929." I was afraid that alcohol might affect his character, but after two beers he did not want any more. My ten-year-old son was in the living room, somewhat timid. At the time he wore his hair in a brush-cut. Paul went up to him, ran his hand through his hair and said, "You're a nice boy, don't let anyone kill you." Clara had prepared a delicious dinner at which he conducted himself perfectly. My arrangement was that I would have him back at the hospital by six o'clock and he was totally cooperative about that. As we passed by the chief's office on the way back to the ward, Jack Hoskins called out, "Hey, Paul! Where have you been?" To which Paul replied, "I've been out in the world."

The next day I said to him, "Why didn't you tell me you liked beer? I would have brought you a bottle now and then." His reply: "No, that would have been against the rules."

Fast forward twenty-seven years - it's the seventy-fifth anniversary of SHNB. I find Paul in a wheelchair; he's an old man. But his smile was the same and he recognized me instantly. "Where are you working now?" I had some treats for him, which he accepted after asking "Why don't you keep them for yourself?" Afterwards, I kicked myself for not bringing him a beer. I was not to see him again.

Chapter 12

All This For Nothing

As it happened, Paul was not the only murderer with whom I got closely involved. One day, word got around that a convicted murderer, who had been sentenced to hang, was in the hospital for a psychiatric evaluation. He was being housed in a small room on 2B, the sick ward, and over the following days probably every staff member found a reason to pass by that room and have a look at him. There was a morbid interest in seeing someone under sentence of death for in those days there were few commutations; most death sentences were carried out.

The person they saw was a slim, dark-haired young fellow with a thin mustache. At the time, he was twenty-one years old. Usually he was engaged in a game of cards or chess with his RCMP guard.

His crime was of the worst kind. While working with a railroad construction gang he had gone out with some other employees in a small town in southern Saskatchewan. Next day the ravaged body of a young girl was found and, before long, it was announced that Guy had been arrested and had confessed. He was sentenced to hang and, after his appeal was rejected, was given a new date with the hangman. It was after this that his lawyer won for him the psychiatric evaluation that was eventually to save his life and have him OIC'd into our hospital "at her majesty's pleasure".

Among the staff there were, expectedly, a number who disagreed with the decision. "The bastard's no crazier than I am," and some never overcame their hostility. Our superintendent was a francophone, as was Guy, and some believed that that circumstance had played a role in the creation of the life-sparing report. I did overhear Dr. Appen, a female doctor from Germany confide to the 2B supervisor, "Doctor Demay said he was worth saving."

There were, in fact, several points in his favour. The morning after the crime he had turned himself in to the police, stating that he had the feeling he might have done something wrong. His family situation was a sad one. He and his two siblings were raised in poverty. His parents had started their family late in life and were in poor health. Since his teenage years Guy had been the main support for his family. He had finished only elementary school.

Guy had stated that he was unaccustomed to drinking and that in the beer parlour of that little town, encouraged by his workmates, he had become intoxicated for the first time in his life, and had blacked out. So, after several interviews with doctors and a battery of psychiatric tests, he was given an alcohol tolerance test. It showed that after a number of drinks he had a total change of character and loss of memory. He was granted a commutation.

Guy was in charge of 8B kitchen, a job that required no more that two or three hours of work each day. We read that Nathan Leopold, during his half-century of incarceration learned several languages to fluency and became a self-taught doctor. Guy also put his time to good use. Almost immediately he began correspondence courses to complete high school and, by concentrated effort, he managed this in less than three years. Since I was doing the same thing, I let him know that he could call on me for help at any time. To my advantage, I used him as another foil in my stumbling efforts to become fluent in French.

He also became interested in music and, using wood from apple boxes, made a violin and a guitar that he learned to play with some degree of proficiency. Jimmy Chrysler, the ward supervisor, was so impressed with his achievements that he prevailed upon the occupational therapy department to give him access to tools and purchased for him any parts that he could not fabricate himself.

Unlike Paul, who for reasons of his own, opened up to me regarding the reasons for his confinement, Guy was silent on the matter and I, of course, never made any effort to bring it up. As far as I was concerned he was a likeable person who was paying dearly for his crime. I agree with Doctor Demay that he was worth saving. What would have been gained by his execution? Certainly, knowing Paul and Guy only served to harden my opposition to capital punishment.

Before I left SHNB I went to say goodbye to Guy. "Just hang in there," I advised, "sooner or later you'll be out of this place." His reply was that he doubted it. "I think I'm here to stay." Eventually he was allowed ground privileges, which we called parole, and completed an apprenticeship with Mr. Balaam in the upholstery shop. The time came when he formed a relationship with a female patient, also on parole, and this situation was apparently tolerated by the institution. They claimed one of the cabins by the river and cultivated a large garden from which they sold produce to staff and visitors. He became a respected and useful member of the hospital community. Over time, his musical abilities flourished to the point where he could play several instruments, including the piano. With other patients and some staff, he formed a band that played at monthly dances, which he organized and where he acted as emcee. I like to think that he was so grateful to the institution for saving his life that he was determined to accept his situation unquestioningly and without complaint. Surely he is an example of what can be accomplished if one has unlimited time and a certain amount of ambition. Eventually, with a new name, he was released into society.

| No Ordinary Job

A friend of mine who had worked at SHNB until retirement filled me in on those details. By coincidence, the same friend ran into him at the Calgary airport some years later. According to him, Guy had married, had children and owned a successful upholstery business.

An intriguing chapter has been added to this story in recent years. A staff member, whose veracity and judgement I respect, was delegated to inform Guy that his younger brother had committed suicide. On receiving this news Guy is reported to have burst out with, "You mean I've gone through all this for nothing!" He explained that he had promised to look after his brother who was in the same work gang. Therefore, he felt obligated to take the blame for a crime of which his brother was actually guilty. Should one give credence to such a story? Certainly, it seems improbable that anyone would be prepared to hold to such a promise to the point of being hanged, or even to bear decades of incarceration. And yet, if there is anything I have learned from my years at SHNB, it is that nothing is beyond the realm of possibility.

Chapter 13

The Elopers

In the euphemistic society that was SHNB patients did not escape or run away - they "eloped". It did not happen very often. The most frequent "elopers" would be recent admissions who had been granted grounds privileges. Since they would invariably head for home, they were easy to locate. In many cases, if it was deemed that the eloper was not a danger to himself or others, they just let him go.

Other patients occasionally slipped away from shops or work gangs. During the summer months complete wards would be taken out to enjoy the sun and fresh air either on walks or simply by relaxing in some grassy area. Occasionally when it came time to go in a patient would "turn up missing" at the count. In these cases the police were informed and it usually wasn't too long before they were back on the ward. Their clothing, behaviour and lack of funds would make them stand out.

Another frequent opportunity for eloping was the North Battleford fair. If the weather was fine, groups of patients with several escorts would be taken to this very popular annual event. It was a duty we detested and tried to avoid. Keeping the group together in the dense crowds was a difficult and nerve-wracking task. It never failed that one of the group would be lost and there would be a frantic search to find him. Actually, it was simply a matter of becoming separated and the patient just as happy to be found as we were to find him. There were, however, real "elopements", but I do not remember that this led to any consequences for the staff. Our supervisors recognized the difficulty of our task.

No Ordinary Job

After eight years at SHNB, I was proud of the fact that no patient had ever eloped on me. Well, this was not strictly true; there was after all, Dunc Hutchins.

Dunc was a resident of what we called the "12" building. It was a three-storey cube separated from the main building and comprising three wards: 12 A, B and C. The patients who lived there were, for the most part, old-timers, who were all on parole, and had the run of the place. They also, to a large degree, ran the place; for among them were farmers, dairymen, gardeners, teamsters and other people with various skills. A good number, probably the majority, were simply housed there, had no duties, were quite content to be living there, and spent their days doing pretty well as they pleased.

Night shift in the 12 building was a one-man job and it was not popular with the staff. Not that it was onerous in any way; in fact, for the most part, there was nothing to do. We were expected to circulate among the sleeping residents two or three times during the night. At five a.m. we had to rouse the "barn gang" for the milking; usually they were already up. These were old farmers with a built-in alarm clock. From that time on it was a turn-around: the patients were in charge of the staff; they did it all. The staff function was only to record the weights of the milk. With our prize herd of Holsteins, production figures were important. As each milker came in he would weigh the milk, give us the number of the cow, and we would record this in the book. We would wonder why these capable and conscientious men were not on their own farms making a living. In many cases a few minutes of conversation would answer that question. People could function quite normally in one sphere, yet be beset with some pretty bizarre delusions in another. But before milking time came the most important task of the night: "the count".

At some point during the night, usually around four a.m., the night supervisor (we called him the chief) would come over for the count. This was not a complicated procedure; we knew how many patients there were on each ward. It was simply a matter of a quick walk through to see that the correct number of beds were occupied and you had your count. On this night I noticed that one bed was empty. There was no need to check the chart to see whose bed it was for on the pillow lay a potato with a feather stuck into it. It was Dunc Hutchins' way of telling us that he had flown.

Dunc had a thing about feathers. His pockets bulged with all kinds of feathers that he had collected over the years. When his clothes were taken for laundering he would transfer his treasure to his clean outfit. He wore an old felt hat and its brim was loaded with a colourful array. As a teamster, one of Dunc's jobs was to bring firewood over from Irrigation for the use of doctors and others who were living in hospital cottages. I had a cousin living in Ibstone and one day he said to me, "I saw a funny thing the other day in the Old Town. A guy had a load of wood on the street for sale, real nice wood, peeled poplar. People wanted to buy it but they were a bit suspicious because the guy had two crow's feathers sticking out of his pipe." It had to be Dunc trying to make a few dollars for himself.

Since there was nothing I could have done to prevent it, Dunc's elopement was not held against me in any way. In fact, Bert Penn, the night chief, was quite nonchalant, "Gone, is he? Guess he wanted a little holiday. He'll be back." And so he was. Sometime later I saw him coming in for lunch. He had a new feather in his hat, a long grey-striped one.

So my record was still unblemished when, on what must have been one of the hottest days of the summer, I was posted to 8A, a ward that would correspond to what we now call long-term care. While many of the patients were bedridden, there were also a good number who were dressed every morning to sit in comfortable chairs in the dayroom. 8A had a side door with a ramp which gave onto a grove of leafy trees that provided welcome shade. There were benches placed haphazardly among the trees and, altogether, it was a pleasant place to spend a hot summer afternoon. Therefore, it was usual to take our patients outside to enjoy the shade and fresh air. Some could make their way out with a bit of support, but most needed to be wheeled out and distributed on the benches. On such a hot day I was quite happy to volunteer to look after them. Every now and then I would take a walk around to see that everyone was all right, but most of the time I did as the patients did, sat back and enjoyed the shade.

The patients usually remained out after shift change, and just before three I made a perfunctory count. I was one short.

Fortunately, it was Maurice who came to relieve me. "I can't find Cornelius," I told him. Maurice could only look at me in disbelief for the patient referred to was not able to walk. "Don't say anything," I continued, "I'll find him."

I made a quick walk through the trees, looking in every spot where he might be hidden, becoming more frantic by the minute. Emerging onto the golf course I looked in all directions but nowhere could he be seen. I was wondering what to do when I was approached by a patient. This patient believed that he was afflicted with an evil eye and, since he was a nice man who did not want to cause harm to anyone, he always carried a piece of cardboard with which he kept the dangerous eye concealed.

"Are you looking for an old man?" he asked. On my affirmative reply he went on, " Well, I saw an old man crawl into that culvert over there," and he pointed to a new steel culvert that had been dumped several hundred feet away.

I hurried over and, sure enough, there was Cornelius hidden a few feet into the corrugated steel culvert. Picking up one end I slid him out and rolled the culvert away.

"Leave me alone!" he cried. "I'm heading for Saskatoon."

Now I was faced with a dilemma. If I left him alone while I went for a wheelchair he could crawl onto the road and be in danger. We were in a dry creek bed and there was a culvert under the road at that point, probably the culvert which was to be replaced. If Cornelius were to crawl into that culvert I would have no option but to get help, and the whole story would become common knowledge. The dressing down which would no doubt follow was not something I would look forward to.

In the end I did something desperate. I was a strong man in those days and I simply hoisted Cornelius up on my shoulders. He was not a small man and, at the moment of doing so, I felt that something had let go inside of me, that I had done myself some harm. Even so I carried him up the slope to a point where it was safe to put him down while I went for a wheelchair. Soon Cornelius was back with his group but not at all happy about it. As for Maurice, I knew he would keep it to himself; I didn't even need to ask.

So I was able to keep my reputation intact, but not without price. It was always my opinion that I had a "cast-iron gut", that I could eat any foods, and in any quantity with no ill effects. But suddenly I began to develop digestive differences. Every meal brought on an attack of indigestion and heartburn, and there were certain foods that I could not tolerate at all. Later, when I was working in a British Columbia psychiatric facility while attending university, these symptoms made a stressful situation even more difficult. First, my doctor recommended that I cut out tea and coffee, and this did seem to reduce the misery, but not for long. My doctor then recommended that I quit smoking and this also had a beneficial, but temporary, effect. Finally, he sent me to a radiologist whose x-rays immediately identified the problem, a severe hiatal hernia. This is a condition where a loop of the stomach works its way up through the diaphragm, and gets caught there, causing acid reflux. It can be difficult to repair and treat. Fortunately, my doctor knew of a surgeon who had had good success with a surgical intervention that he had developed. Medicare was still a few years in the future and my experience illustrates how things used to be before this great boon became part of Canadian life.

Dr. Robin didn't beat about the bush, "You need this operation, but how do you intend to pay for it?"

I informed him that I belonged to Gems, an excellent medical plan which the British Columbia Government maintained for its employees.

"That's good," he said and went on to explain. "This is a big operation, the only one I'll do that day, so I don't want my fee to be paid in dribs and drabs. If you didn't have a plan I would put you on a special diet, and you would have to sleep on a slanted bed."

I was already existing on hot milk and crackers, the only food I could tolerate, so what his special diet might have consisted of I could not begin to guess.

The operation was scheduled for the day after I had written my last exam at university. It took place at the Burnaby General Hospital and I was on a gurney, already dozey after a shot of Demerol, when I was awakened by a green-gowned female doctor. "I'm Doctor Wilson," she announced, "I'll be doing your anaesthetic. What arrangements have you made to pay my bill?"

"I belong to Gems," I managed to reply.

"Do you know your number?" she asked.

I didn't know it by heart, and all I could do was assure her the surgeon had all my information, and that seemed to satisfy her. It must not have been an easy thing for her to do, and it illustrates that medicare transformed life not only for the patient, but for the doctor as well. Certainly, I had nothing but respect for all the doctors involved and I understand their positions perfectly. I respected them all the more when the operation turned out to be a complete success.

In sum, my determination to "save face" cost me dearly. On my chest I wear a twelve-inch scar; internally I have a severed vagus nerve and alterations to my stomach. Add to this the years of pain and discomfort that I had to tolerate.

"You had a big tear in your diaphragm," the surgeon informed me. "You must have done some heavy lifting at sometime."

But I took comfort in the fact that no one was able to say about me, "The only patient who ever ran away on him couldn't walk."

Another benefit is that I never took up smoking again.

If there was anyone who might be termed an "escape artist" it was Edwin Lauritzen. He had eloped several times, usually from walks or on occasions when a ward would be taken out on the lawn or on the golf course to enjoy the summer sun. We had been warned about him, "He can run like a rabbit. If he runs you won't catch him; just try to see where he goes." Usually he would be found before too long since, after the initial spurt, he would find a secluded spot, strip, and take a catatonic, unmoving stance.

No Ordinary Job

I never heard him speak, but when you looked at him, it was obvious there was an active mind at work. The couple of times when I had him out for walks he was interesting to watch. He knew that we were uneasy, and he made it a sort of a game. He would look at us with a kind of smirk as though to say, "I'll take off when I feel like it." A small man, his walk would win the Monty Python's Ministry of Funny Walks. Each stride was as long as his legs would allow.

Once he got away and was not found before nightfall. His family and the police were notified, and a search initiated without success. Then, a couple of days later, a farmer working his fields was shocked to see a naked man standing like a statue at the edge of a bluff. He was brought back to the hospital covered with mosquito bites, starved and dehydrated. It took a couple of weeks on 2B, with intravenous feeding and special diet to restore him to relative good health.

His story had a sad ending. It happened after I left SHNB, but I was apprised of the details. For a good while, after the previous escape, he was kept confined to a locked ward. However, finally compassion ruled and he was transferred to a ward where he could take part in the usual recreational activities. There he seemed to be functioning well, until, one day, he took off from a walking group and could not be found. After several days the search was called off and the general consensus was that he had gone into the river. It was all resolved a couple of years later when skeletal remains were found in some bushes several miles from the hospital. It was Edwin, he had finally got away for good.

Chapter 14

The Wrong House

Although 6A was termed the "refractory ward" it did not follow that the patients were dangerous or hard to manage. The population of the hospital, at that time, remained relatively constant and empty beds were few. A disappointing few did not return to normalcy and while their more flamboyant symptoms may have diminished they were often deemed incapable of functioning outside, and ended up becoming permanent residents.

Alan Dewer was a patient who, as far as I knew, had never been "difficult". He did, however, have a history of trying to "elope". During one such attempt he had jumped from a dangerous height and sustained serious injuries to his right leg. As a result he was not able to bend his right knee and walked with a pronounced limp. I noticed him the first time I was booked to 6A; there were several reasons why he stood out. Although sallow-complected, he would be considered quite good-looking. As well, he kept himself neat and well groomed. However, what placed him apart was that he radiated intelligence and alertness. He never conversed at any length, but I often noticed him when I had occasion to pass by the basement workshops. Because of his handicap he could not be part of any outside "gang", but at various times I would see him in the shoe-repair shop, or the book bindery, or the kitchen. He had a reputation as a good worker.

As I entered my third year at SHNB our personal financial situation, though still precarious, became less desperate. Our boy, at more than two years old, was no longer a baby. Since we had not had any sort of holiday during all that time we decided that we would splurge and

No Ordinary Job

take a trip to Saskatoon on my two days off. After all our deprivation we were quite excited as we sat in the Greyhound on a beautiful summer morning. At the last moment, who should board the bus but Alan Dewer. His face, on seeing me, was the picture of dismay; one could almost see in a balloon above his head, "what rotten, stinking luck!" He took the seat immediately behind the driver, which allowed him to extend his ankylosed right leg into the aisle. An hour later we were in Radisson, where we planned to stop on our way back. Not long after we were crossing the South Saskatchewan River at Borden, where Clara exclaimed at the beauty of the valley. There was only a short stop at the next town, Langham, and just as the driver was about to set off, Alan pulled himself from his seat and vaulted out the door. Since he almost certainly had a ticket to Saskatoon, this took the driver by surprise, but he only shook his head and drove on.

As for me, I knew exactly what caused him to act in that way. He was afraid that at the busy Saskatoon bus depot I would find some way to draw attention to him. He had no way of knowing that, although it was probably my duty, I had no intention of doing anything of the sort. By leaving the bus in that small town, where a stranger would immediately attract interest, he would certainly reduce his chances of getting away. At any rate, it was not long before the police brought him back, and it was not long before he was gone again, and this time it would be for good.

After ten years at SHNB I had resigned and moved to British Columbia with the intention of attending university there. I chose B.C. because it was possible to work in some mental health facility and attend university courses at the same time. As a Saskatchewan-trained psych nurse I was hired immediately by the B.C. Department of Health, and I will always be grateful for the way I was treated by B.C. administrators who did everything I could ask for to make it possible for me to achieve my goal. For four years I was able to work the night shift so I could attend classes during the day. Even after graduation, while teaching school, I was able to work during my summer holidays as summer relief. Teachers' salaries were nothing to be proud of at that time and, with student loans and other expenses, I was not able to save enough to cover the two unpaid months of summer break. The first year I worked in a geriatric ward, work which I knew well. The second summer it was Crease Clinic, the principal active treatment ward, which made for a satisfying and enjoyable two months. The third summer I found myself posted to Riverside, the forensic unit. There were housed, under very tight security, the murderers, serial rapists and other offenders whose trials I had followed in the news, and who had been found insane. Others had been transferred from prisons after developing mental illness there. Without going into too much detail, suffice to say that it was a terrible place to work, and the experience discouraged me from ever applying for summer relief again.

It was on my first day there, in fact only a few minutes after I entered the place that I was surprised to hear someone calling my name, "...what are you doing here?" The question came from a stocky, balding individual seated among a couple of dozen others in a dayroom. "I remember you from North Battleford," he went on to explain. "My name's Alan Dewer."

"Alan, for gosh sakes!" I exclaimed. "I sure do remember you. I didn't recognize you; it's been a long time."

Before the day was out I knew how he had spent the years since I had last seen him. After his "elopement" he had somehow found his way to Texas, where he spent many years. It is a testament to his intelligence that he was able to bamboozle welfare authorities there. Not only did he succeed in drawing social assistance, but he also received, at state expense, an operation on his knee, which gave him some movement in that joint, and, although he still had a limp, improved his mobility significantly.

Apart from simply being there, and thus maintaining order and protecting the residents from each other, there was not a great deal for the staff to do. Therefore, we were encouraged to socialize with the residents and elicit their comments and complaints. Consequently, I was able to spend a lot of time with Alan, and it was time well spent. His intelligence and powers of observation had allowed him to "take a read" on patients and I was quite prepared to accept his advice on how to deal with various individuals in a way which would avoid conflict and encourage cooperation. Over time, he revealed to me the events that led to his being confined in the forensic unit.

It was never made clear why he left Texas and found his way to British Columbia, although there was some suggestion that political changes made it more difficult to qualify for social assistance. At any rate he had no difficulty getting on the welfare rolls in Vancouver. He lived, like hundreds of others, in a cheap room in the Skid Road area. It must have been a depressing and lonely life since he was not a part of the alcohol or drug culture. In fact, he was not even a smoker.

So he would have been easily tempted into the situation which was to lead him afoul of the law and, ultimately, into Riverside.

It happened on "welfare Wednesday" which was the day welfare cheques were issued once a month. It was a day when drunkenness and disorder reigned on Skid Road. In the lineup to receive his cheque, Alan happened to find himself behind a large black man who was accompanied by two aboriginal women. Before long a deal was struck.

"If you buy the booze, we can have a party and one of these girls can be your girlfriend for the night."

It was boredom and the hunger for companionship, rather than the alcohol and promise of feminine company that led Alan to agree. Before long they were on their way in a taxi, first to a liquor store where a good supply of beer and other "booze" was acquired, then to a dwelling a few blocks away where the supplies were unloaded. It was then that Alan's hopes for a sociable evening were dashed. His erstwhile host turned to him with words that were far from welcoming. "Thanks a lot, sucker. Now fuck off!" When Alan objected, he was kicked down a short flight of stairs, landing ignonimously on his back. Fortunately, apart from his pride, he was unhurt.

Distressed and disappointed he returned to his lonely room, but not to sleep. All night it gnawed at him, the unfairness of it all. "He even made me carry in all the booze before he kicked me out." He decided he was not going to take it lying down. He found a pop bottle and somehow convinced a filling station to sell him a few cents worth of gasoline. He then went in search of the house where he had been so poorly treated, splashed the gasoline over the back porch and set it alight. Immediately the shocked homeowner came out and Alan realized that he was at the wrong house. The owner, with his garden hose, quickly doused the flames while Alan, knowing the jig was up, limped off to a nearby café, ordered a coffee, and waited for the inevitable. A few minutes later he saw the homeowner, accompanied by a policeman, pointing him out through the café window. When he appeared in court it was not difficult to convince the judge that his bizarre behaviour qualified him for Riverside.

The wry humour and self-deprecation he displayed in telling me the story made him appear quite normal in my eyes. I felt that anyone hearing his story in the way he told it would say, "There's not too much wrong with this guy."

On my last day there I left him my phone number with the usual perfunctory message, "Call me if you need anything." More than two years passed and then one evening I was surprised to receive a phone call from him. He informed me that he had been released and was living in Vancouver.

"Come and see me the next time you're in Vancouver."

Naturally I was curious to see him again and the very next weekend we drove to the city for expressly that purpose. We found the address he had given in a quite respectable area of Vancouver. However, his lodgings were anything but inviting. Several steps led down to a door, which opened to a low, dingy basement. Along the right wall the owner had hammered in a couple of rooms to rent out for extra income. It would be difficult to believe they could have passed any kind of inspection. In Alan's room, a tiny window let in so little light that the single hanging light bulb had to be on constantly. Forced-air heating came from a duct situated directly above the bed. The cooking facilities consisted of a two-burner hotplate sitting on a ledge formed by the top of the foundation. There was no table, nor were there chairs; the size of the room did not allow for any such luxuries.

These circumstances meant that he had to spend all his time reclining on his bed and it was from there that he entertained us, while we leaned against the wall. There was no way he could have offered us any kind of refreshment. Fortunately, Clara had brought a box of baked goods of various kinds and they were much appreciated.

As for Alan, had I passed him on the street I would not have recognized him. He seemed thinner. He was now completely bald, but as though to compensate, he sported a bushy black beard. We found him quite entertaining, jocular and still possessed of the wry sense of humour which had impressed me at Riverside. From his conversation we gathered that he spent a lot of time using his bus pass to explore the city and made good use of the library. It seemed he seldom cooked anything in his room, taking most of his meals in fast-food facilities. Only one block from Alan's room there was a well-established restaurant called Helen's and he told us that he occasionally had breakfast or lunch there. Suddenly he said, "I want to take you out to lunch at Helen's. OK?" Although we tried to avoid coming to Vancouver unless it was absolutely necessary we didn't have the heart to refuse him, and we set a date.

    Thus, a few days later we went again to his room to find that he remembered his invitation and was waiting for us. It was summer and in his tan slacks and light windbreaker he looked quite smartly turned out. In the restaurant the waitress greeted him warmly by name and we spent a thoroughly enjoyable couple of hours.

    Although he seemed to be functioning quite well, there was something about him that I found disquieting. He talked about a cashier at Woodwards, as well as a waitress at Helen's whom he considered his girlfriends. He had been released with a three-month supply of medication, a minimum dose of Thorazine. His admission that he took it only sporadically, "I take it when I think of it," was a definite cause for worry.

    Nothing more was heard from him and of course he had no phone. On a rainy December day Clara and I had reason to be in Vancouver.

    "Let's go see if Alan is still in the same place," I suggested.

    He was still in the same place but he was not the same man. The person who greeted us had a straggly beard and unkempt strands of hair reached to his shoulders. He had apparently decided to assert his Jewishness, a decision that had created mysterious enemies. Somewhere he had obtained a light bulb of which the filament was in the shape of the Star of David. Every now and then he would reach up and flick his Star of David light on and off exclaiming with a triumphant laugh, "That'll stop them!" The tenant in the adjoining room had left his door open. Obviously a lover of music, he had an elaborate sound system composed of several speakers, turntables and tape recorders.

"This guy's a German," confided Alan. "He thinks he can read my mind, but he doesn't know I can cut him off."

There was a rancid smell in his room. The heating duct above his bed was covered by a piece of cardboard and sealed shut with tape due to his suspicion that he was being "gassed". His heat now came from his hotplate which stood on its side. Beside it was a fry pan containing a thickness of congealed fat. In the course of our conversation Alan revealed that for reasons of safety he seldom left his room. On his last outing he had purchased a large quantity of ground beef that he kept in a black plastic bag hanging from the branch of a tree in the backyard.

To see him in this condition was a shock and a disappointment. It was not so much his behaviour that I found frightening. It was the fact that this man, whom I had come to consider relatively normal and under control, could in such a short time develop such marked paranoid symptomology.

Once again I blamed the system. While it might be an admirable concept to try to place psychiatric patients in the community, to live free, Alan's case was a classic example of how it should not be done. Obviously, no one had been checking on him. Lonely and friendless in his dank and dismal room, his defenses broke down and he fell into his psychotic state.

But now I found myself faced with a dilemma. Every instinct and knowledge gained by experience told me that it was not possible to just walk away from the situation.

"I've got to turn him in," I said to my wife. "He can't go on living like that. And he might end up doing some harm to the guy in the next room."

Easier said than done. It took innumerable phone calls to various agencies before I was connected to a suspicious individual who identified himself as the social worker in charge of Alan's case.

"How do you know this man?" he asked.

I tried to explain my long history with Alan but he remained skeptical. Finally, I put an end to it, "I'm telling you the truth. Alan is not capable of looking after himself, and he is a danger to his neighbor. You can decide what to do."

I heard no more but he must have been picked up because I had no more contact with him. It was about a year later, on Christmas Eve actually, that Clara answered the phone, "Someone wants to talk to you," she said, passing me the phone.

It was Alan, "You have to help me. They gave me a room across from the police station and the police are spying on me." I was blunt with him, perhaps too blunt, "Alan, the police and not spying on you. Stay in that room." Before I could say more he hung up.

At times I regret that I was so abrupt, but I could not advise him otherwise. What became of him after that must remain a mystery for I never saw or heard of him again.

No Ordinary Job

Certainly, he was an interesting man, and his was an interesting case. His diagnosis was "schizophrenia undifferentiated", and it is not surprising that his doctor found it difficult to make an accurate assessment. In some ways he was another "broken reed". He took pride in the fact that, in his entire life, he had never held a job. For some reason he had in intense hatred for his father. He told me that he once saw his father in Saskatoon but did not approach him. "I saw the old bastard on the other side of the street but he didn't know I was there." This must have happened after his last successful "elopement" from SHNB. Somehow, he was able to find his way to Texas, and I regret now that I did not make a greater effort to find out how he managed to do it.

Chapter 15

Shanghai

The causes of mental illness remain, still to this day, largely a mystery and even well into the twentieth century there was a certain primitiveness about the kinds of treatment available and the cure-rate remained discouragingly low. Treatment was often reactive, treating the symptoms first. A patient coming in with aggressive or combative behaviour or extreme agitation would be isolated and calmed down with restraint, electric shock and sedation. After that the options were limited. There was no time in SHNB for anything fancy. Psychoanalysis was not on the agenda although we did hear from time to time that one of the doctors had taken a special interest in a patient to the point of finding the time to do something Freudian.

During the early 50's the treatment of choice was electric shock. As described in our lectures, it had been noticed that epileptics, after a grand mal seizure, often appeared calmer and more relaxed. While this may only have been a natural aftermath to what must be a traumatic and exhausting blow to the body, doctors desperate to find a way to treat mental illness decided to try to recreate the convulsions and loss of consciousness in the hopes of benefitting their patients. The results were good enough to make electro-convulsive therapy (ECT) the most common treatment for decades. Some patients were "cured" in the sense that they were discharged and remained discharged. Others were helped in the sense that they could be discharged for a period of time or were able to live comfortably.

So, three times a week, there would be a line-up of patients waiting for shocks. They were new admissions as well as patients who had "gone up the pole" or become depressed on other wards. There could not be much finesse about it; patients were led in and placed on the table, shocked and removed in almost assembly-line fashion. The few who resisted were simply man-handled into place. The speed and efficiency with which it was done was likely beneficial, for, on reflection, I can't imagine how terrifying it must have been.

Shock treatment has always intrigued me and it is something I have thought about time and again. Why was there so little resistance to what must have been a terrifying situation? Imagine the scene: you are brought into a room, directed to lie on a bed surrounded by four men who immediately lean on you, holding down your body and immobilizing your limbs. This could not be a prelude to anything pleasant.

Any of the strong young men who went through it could have caused a real scene. Yet in the hundreds of times I took part in electroshock therapy treatment there was never anything more than minimal or symbolic resistance. Was it simply a matter of resignation - an acceptance of the fact that resistance, in the end, was futile?

In our group we came to believe, and hope, that it was not as unpleasant and frightening as it appeared. We liked to think that it was like going under anaesthetic – the next thing you know you wake up in your bed, the operation is over and you have survived. A comforting thought, but then there was the shout. It was never absent and everything about it suggested protest. Was it perhaps the body's unconscious response to this profound insult to its very centre?

Nevertheless, shock treatment was, statistically, safe. During my time at SHNB we lost only one patient in shock. He was a young fellow who had been born lacking ear lobes. He had only openings into his skull. It was especially tragic in that he foresaw his fate. An educated, intelligent man, he knew what shock treatment involved, in which respect he differed from the majority of patients. He stated to Maurice, "This is going to kill me. I know it." And it did. On receiving his first shock he went into immediate arrest and nothing could be done to help him. One can only imagine what a shattering result this must have been for his family.

Shock is still used on a limited basis, since it is sometimes the most effective treatment for certain conditions. In the 1960's I assisted with ECT at Crease Clinic in B.C. The patients were given a mild anaesthetic and an injection of curare to lessen the severity of convulsions.

Much has been written about the effects of electro shock on the brain and on memory with opinions varying from permanent damage to no harm. Intellectually, I had been of the opinion that some damage had to take place. It just seemed logical that this would be so. However, I was witness to a test which, while not scientific in any sense of the word, was surprising in the extreme.

"Shanghai", one of our long-term patients, had probably never been near that metropolis. Given the history of Chinese immigration to Canada, he was probably from Canton province (now Guandong). Still, somehow he had that name pinned on him and he was addressed in no other way. Shanghai's dubious claim to fame was that he had undergone shock treatment a greater number of times than any other patient, in fact more times than any of the old staff could remember. When I left SHNB he was already well into the two hundreds, and I was told that his final tally was around three hundred treatments.

No Ordinary Job

Shanghai was also unusual in that he truly welcomed shock. Following a course of eight or twelve treatments he would have a period of relative normalcy. Then gradually his demons would take possession of him; he would become extremely agitated fighting the enemies that only he could see. He would come to the shock room practically on the run and jump up on the table willingly and, one would say, gratefully.

During a visit to the hospital a quarter century later, in my tour of the wards I found Shanghai already in bed. Like many Asiatics he did not seem to have aged much. What is more, his psychoses seem to have "burnt out" as he had not had shock for a long time. What I saw before me was a perfectly normal seeming man like any other. He gave us a questioning look – no doubt wondering what this strange couple wanted from him. "Hello Shanghai, how are you doing?" He looked at me for a time and then said in perfect English, "I remember you, what's your name?" When he heard who I was he accepted my name, "Skalazub – Skalazub. Yes, I remember you. Where do you live now?" My wife, who speaks Chinese, spoke to him in Cantonese and Mandarin but he only shook his head. Through lack of use he had lost his native tongue.

Seeing Shanghai again had the effect of adding another to my list of regrets. I remember how Shanghai, after his treatment, would sort of hover around where staff might be grouped, with a sort of expectant air. Now I realized that he was wanting some normalcy, some attention. Why didn't I take the trouble to talk to him – maybe get his help with some task? Regrets, I have many.

Insulin shock was done on ward 4B, a bright new ward with special amenities. Besides the TV and stereo, there was a billiard table, table tennis and a little side room where patients could make a cup of tea or coffee and store things in a fridge. A limited number of patients could be handled there, and doctors seemed to choose patients who were special in some way: perhaps in their education, or work history, or family situation. Possibly because the "raw material" we started with was superior the success rate was high. As well, patients undergoing this therapy seemed to achieve an improvement in physical health.

The treatment was onerous and required close supervision with a doctor present throughout. First, the patient, lying comfortably in his bed was administered a large injection of insulin sufficient to, almost immediately, put him into a coma. This state of unconsciousness was accompanied by convulsions of varying degrees of severity. Certain patients convulsed so violently that they needed to be strapped down to avoid injury; with some there would only be a slight tremor. Some patients vocalized in various ways, most were silent.

At the end of a set period, usually thirty minutes, glucose was injected to bring the patient out of his coma. It was almost miraculous to see the result.

Sadly, on two occasions this miracle did not occur, and the patients succumbed to what was called irreversible coma. The first was a fellow just out of his teens, and in his first year at university. The second was a handsome, well-built teacher of Ukrainian descent. An air gunner during the war, he was a member of the Caterpiller club, a select group whose members had parachuted from crashing bombers over occupied Europe. This loss, which occurred during his last scheduled treatment was a shock to all who knew him and left a pall over the whole hospital.

And that was the end of it. The decision was made to put an end to insulin shock. It was history.

As it happened, the final months of I.S.T. coincided with the appearance of Dr. Matheu, who had been given an office in 4B. He had been involved with LSD treatment somewhere and it was planned that he would begin experimental treatments with LSD with selected patients. From this came about the creation of psycho-drama. One of the female staff with a flair for the dramatic was enrolled to assist Dr. Matheu in this treatment. It was a learn-as-you-go situation. Some event from the patient's history that might be traumatic such as a divorce, an infidelity or a death would be acted out with the patient who had been injected with LSD. Ward staff would be roped in to take part, in many cases without much enthusiasm. My impression was that the success rate was not too impressive with the possible exception of alcoholics who seemed to benefit from the treatment.

I have to digress here to narrate an event that certainly qualifies for the term mind-boggling. More than thirty years later in Reno, Nevada I was taking part in a Scrabble tournament. I came to be matched against an opponent who was a tiny woman of advanced years in a powered wheel chair. As often happened, after we introduced ourselves we sought to get to know each other. She asked where I was from and I told her Canada. She informed me that she lived in Indiana.

"But I lived in Canada for a while," she said "in Saskatchewan. Have you ever been there?"

Further questioning brought out that she had lived in North Battleford and that her husband was a doctor at the mental hospital. It was then that I looked at her nametag and realized that she was the wife, widow actually, of Dr. Matheu. Apparently Dr. Matheu had died some years before and she was living in a retirement centre where Scrabble was a favourite pastime. She played a good game – her mind was as sharp as anyone's. She wanted news about some of the people she knew when she was living in hospital housing. Later, when I had a chance I mentioned her to some of her former neighbours who remembered a tiny Asian woman of extreme beauty.

But, what struck me about this was how it stretched coincidence to the nth degree. She from Indiana, me from B.C., meeting at a Scrabble tournament in Reno to talk about life in a small corner of Saskatchewan 30 years before. The odds against such a thing happening are hard to imagine!

Chapter 16

A Narrow Escape

A question frequently asked of psych nurses was, "Aren't you afraid?" or "How do staff control a ward full of mental patients?" In truth, there was not much control necessary. Psychiatric patients, thankfully, do not collude; each man is "a world unto himself". Except on admission or active treatment wards, patients rarely communicated with each other, and I could not say that I ever saw anything resembling a friendship develop between two patients. On rare occasions when a patient might become agitated, "go up the pole" in hospital vernacular, and attack the staff, he could expect no support from other patients. The exception might be with psychopathic patients, of which we had a few. These, however, were skillfully distributed around the wards so that no ganging up could take place. In fact, on the night shift, a single staff would be posted to the parole building, which housed in the neighbourhood of three hundred patients.

Occasionally, or rather, rarely, an aggressive patient would be brought in by the police, handcuffed and resistive. The policy with such a patient was to overwhelm him with sufficient staff, give him a shock or a shot and place him in a unit.

In enlightened Saskatchewan police involvement in patient admissions was discouraged. For this reason SHNB had its own ambulance which was dispatched to pick up patients anywhere in the province. All grads were eventually rotated to a month of escort duty. If the pick-up was in some far corner of the province this would, occasionally, entail an overnight trip.

The odd time there would be a violent pick-up, usually from a hospital lock-up. In such cases the escort nurse could call on police for assistance while the patient was injected with a sedative and restrained on a stretcher.

Staff looked forward to escort duty as a break from the usual routine. As for me, I did it twice, and found it tense and stressful. I was always relieved when my month was over. As might be expected, things did not always go well and a good number of these horror stories became part of SHNB lore.

I was never a fighter, never felt that my six-foot plus size gave me any advantage. In my entire life I had never had to become engaged in a physical confrontation with another person. I even managed to avoid the schoolboy scraps which were so commonplace. How unusual this is, I could not say. Certainly, in my years at sea, and at other jobs, I witnessed several fights take place, and the brouhahas my workmates got involved in were frequent topics of conversation and boasting. If the raconteur's story was backed up by bodily evidence, such as a black eye, this made him all the more worthy of respect and admiration.

My non-assertive character and instinct for self-preservation no doubt stood me in good stead during my years at SHNB. One incident, however, still comes back to haunt me after the passage of half a century.

It was one of those occasions when there was a staff shortage. It was the night shift and, as a grad, I was posted alone to be in charge of 2A, the admissions ward. This was not unusual, since it was not anticipated that there would be any trouble on 2A. Patients who might have been difficult should have been sorted out and placed in units or sedated. So, as a rule, one could expect a quiet night of reading and trying to stay awake.

No Ordinary Job

On relieving the afternoon staff I was informed that the police had brought in a new patient that afternoon.

"It's that guy walking around over there. He keeps getting up all the time. He's already had a second Seconal so he should flake out pretty soon."

During the night shift the office and dispensary were closed, and the staff on duty sat at a small table in the corridor. The new patient returned to his bed, but it was not long before he came out again and started pacing up and down the corridor. He was dressed in a hospital nightgown and one could see he was a strong, muscular man. He had been working out daily, of course not in a gym, but in the fields, hefting bales of hay and scoops of grain. I was clearly no match for him physically.

I spoke to him a couple of times, "George, why don't you lie down and try to sleep?" His answer was to give me a look that I interpreted as challenging; certainly he made me apprehensive. The chief, Sparky Clifford came by on his rounds and asked, "Why don't you tell that guy to go to bed?"

"There's something about him that makes me nervous," I was not ashamed to reply. "I'm going to leave him strictly alone." Fortunately, the chief let me have my way.

It was a long and nerve-wracking night. The patient kept up his pacing the whole time; almost certainly he had only pretended to swallow the Seconal. I pretended to read but there were not too many pages turned. Seven o'clock finally came and I never was more relieved to go home and let the day staff take over.

The following night I found out what had happened after I left. It was decided to take the patient to a unit. It took six men to do it. Watches and glasses were broken, uniforms torn to shreds, a couple of staff members were nursing injuries. I realized that my instincts had saved me from serious injury, perhaps even death. Had I touched him in any way he would certainly have attacked me. I would have been no match for him, and had the attack taken place in the dorm I would have had no way to summon help. It was a narrow escape and the most dangerous situation I was ever faced with at SHNB.

As for the patient, after a few shocks he became a ward favourite, a most likeable and gentle person, friendly, smiling, always willing to help with ward routine. He, himself, came to laugh at the delusions that led to his admission. For some reason he had come to believe that he was being forced to marry the "town bike". I had a married sister who lived in his area and the woman in question was once pointed out to me. I thought she was quite attractive.

His stay with us was not long, relatively speaking. After about three months he went home. Sadly, his illness must have been deeper than it appeared. On a cold winter day he took his rifle and made his way to an empty granary at the back of the farm. There he ended his life. As word of his death spread throughout the wards, all who had known him were saddened and disappointed.

In all my years working on psychiatric wards I was struck only once, and the injury I sustained was hardly worthy of the term. What made it unique was that the offender was one of the "originals". Henri Martin was one of the transferees from Manitoba when SHNB was opened in 1914. He would have been in his late seventies or even eighties, classified as a bed patient but still ambulant. One morning I was bringing him his breakfast tray; he was still asleep, facing away from me. I gave his shoulder a little shake, "Wake up Henri. Breakfast!" In one move he flipped over and landed me a punch right to the mouth. The result was a split lip and a good lesson. We had been taught to

No Ordinary Job

avoid making sudden moves, especially when dealing with catatonics. I tried to never leave myself vulnerable again.

There was one comical incident when a patient grabbed me by my tie. It happened to be on a day when I had decided to wear a "clip-on", and it came off in his hand. Anybody could have read the expression on his face "Hey, not fair!" Not long after we received our new uniforms and neckties became a thing of the past.

Chapter 17

They're Not Crazy

I was booked on 2B, the sickward, on afternoons and had just walked on the ward when Lou Stiles called out, "Ed, they're short on 6A. You'll fill in there today."

Arriving on 6A I immediately noticed two patients who were new to me. They were unusual in that they seemed so young. And, since they were rather small in stature the thought "a couple of kids" came to my mind. They were good-looking boys; one was blond and walked with a limp, the other was brown-haired. One walked on one side of the corridor, one on the other. I noticed that a patient walking between them displayed some nervousness.

The supervisor, Lou Gubbe, told me that they had been brought in by the police the day before after they had a run-in with a neighbor who accused them of throwing stones at his ducks.

"Boy, they're tough," said Lou Gubbe, "all the guys were scared of them so we had to straighten them out a bit. Don't let them get away with anything. Once they found out they could have all the tobacco they wanted, and didn't need to take it from somebody, they settled down."

They came from an area that was quite remote and were not attending school. Although their English was adequate they spoke to each other in Ukrainian, probably to avoid being understood. Most of the time, however, they communicated in a language of their own composed of monosyllables, grunts, facial expressions and signals. Their upbringing had been deprived and primitive, with a motherless home and an uncaring, alcoholic father. The diagnosis they received was something catch-all like "anti-social personality", but the doctor said, "They're not crazy, they're just uncivilized."

So the only treatment they received was recreational and occupational therapy and the socialization which accompanied these activities. A program was initiated to "civilize" them. They were enrolled in correspondence courses with the primary goal of improving their reading, writing and math skills of which they had barely the rudiments. Their education was supervised by the psychology department and, while they showed no great enthusiasm for their lessons, they didn't rebel against their daily routine.

When Robert and Edwin arrived at SHNB they were sixteen and seventeen years old respectively. At the end of the almost two years they spent with us they had filled out, become huskier and, from an educational point of view, were better prepared for life. I never heard of them having any visitors, nor did they have anyone to speak for them. In the hospital they formed no friendships, remained aloof, separate. But between themselves the bond had become stronger; they moved and thought as one person.

Since there was no reason to hold them, and since there seemed to be no one willing to be responsible for them, they were finally discharged into the care of Social Welfare in North Battleford. Some time later we heard that one of them had been charged with forging a cheque, which might be considered a testament to the quality of education they received at SHNB. How this was resolved, I never did learn.

It must have been a year or so after their release that Clara and I, with another couple, were having a beer at the Auditorium Hotel. Suddenly we became aware of a commotion – a couple of waiters were trying to eject Edwin for some reason. They didn't realize what they were up against. Ripped off shirt buttons were flying like machine gun bullets. A woman at a nearby table caught a salt shaker to the head sustaining a nasty cut. It took several staff and a couple of customers to finally subdue Edwin and hold him down until the police could cuff him and take him out, fighting all the way. Since neither the fracas nor its consequences were reported in the press, there was no way of knowing how Edwin came out of it.

It was some years later that his name leapt out at me from the pages of the Vancouver Sun. Apparently Edwin was a guest at a party in a west-end highrise and he got the notion to enter a neighbouring apartment by walking along a ledge on the outside of the building. He fell many storeys to instant death. Since that was the only way I ever knew them I assumed that the brothers were together when the event took place, and imagined how terrible it must have been for the surviving brother. Then came 2004, Saskatchewan's centennial year. Every town, village and municipality published a history in which the original families and pioneers were honoured. In a short history about the boys' family I discovered that Robert had died before Edwin. No details were given. What it meant was that both brothers were dead before the age of thirty. Where did the hospital, which played such a large role in their lives, fail? Certainly not from lack of effort; probably their early mistreatment, compounded by the ill effects of alcohol abuse had contributed to their early demise.

Chapter 18

Messiah God King

Ward 8B was supervised by Jimmy Chrysler, another "prince of a man". Calm, scholarly, respectful, he elicited maximum effort from his staff. It was not an easy ward, but it was a happy one.

The first time I was posted to 8B, about half its population was made up of TB patients who required special care and protective measures on the part of the nursing staff. Not long after, all TB patients were transferred to Weyburn, where a ward had been created for TB patients only.

So 8B became a mixed ward, populated, for the most part by bed patients, many of whom had grown old in the hospital. It would be similar to the extended care wings, which have now become part of many general hospitals. There were also a couple of dozen older patients who were still quite mobile, many of whom could go downstairs for their meals. These people spent their days seated comfortably in a large, airy dayroom. Among them resided a patient who was a favourite of all staff there, and especially of our "gang of four". We made use of every opportunity to spend time talking to him, and listening to his wisdom.

His name was Robert Alexander McGregor, but that was only part of his title. A new staff posted to the ward would find himself sternly corrected if he were to say, "Lunch time, Mister McGregor."

"Nay, Mister. Messiah God King, Robert Alexander McGregor."

Often a staff, passing through the ward, just to brighten his day would call out a greeting, "Hello, Mac!" just to hear the response, "Nay Mac. Messiah God King, Robert Alexander McGregor." He covered all the bases.

At the time he was probably in his late fifties, of medium height, somewhat portly, with thinning grey hair. Everything about him: his comportment, his speech, his expression, demonstrated that he took his status as "ruler of the world" very seriously. No matter how ill fitting were the clothes he was issued, he managed to make himself look neat and presentable. Like everyone else, he had to make do with a pair of denim trousers and a work shirt. His shirt was always buttoned to the neck, and his pants, no matter how many sizes too big, would be made to fit by clever over-lapping and tucking. Most staff, out of respect for his position, would make an effort to pick out a good set for him.

Sometime in the past Jimmy Chrysler had somehow obtained for him a large, padded, brown leatherette armchair. From this throne he would survey his realm. Occasionally on returning from his meal, or from the washroom he would find some patient, out of temerity or ignorance, occupying his chair. He made short work of that; a curt "Begone!" would send the poor subject, and we were all his subjects, scurrying away.

Never smiling, always with a stern and serious mien, his was a rule of iron. If he became annoyed, (it had to be staff annoying him - other patients left him alone) he was quick to show his displeasure. Like all royalty, he hated to be touched. Sometimes staff would become overly familiar, "You ticklish, Mac?" and poke him in the chest, or perhaps rub his head. It took only a few utterances of "Begone!" or "Desist!" before he would lose all patience and go into the punishment mode, "Remove that skull!" or "Scrap that cranium!" The fact that no servant materialized to fulfill his dictates did not seem to concern him or discourage him. He had issued his decree and he expected it would be carried out.

On one occasion we brought a female subject before him for judgement - Althea Watts, one of my classmates. We accused her of all-night carousing, cavorting, neglecting her children and consorting with disreputable men. The unusual situation seemed to disconcert him. He seemed to display more anger than usual. Finally he shouted, arm upraised, "Banish her to one of the Outer Islands!" I wondered whether this Augustean sentence would apply only to females, but no, during the years I was to hear it imposed on male miscreants as well.

Among our group of four we cultivated him like a precious resource. Maurice and Bill both carried little notebooks in which they jotted down his most memorable utterances. If I happened to spot him downstairs at mealtimes, or even while passing through the ward, I would stop and inquire, "Greetings, your majesty, how goes the realm?" His answer was optimistic and unchanging, "The realm prospers. The subjects are content. All is well." In the dayroom his throne was opposite to a mentally-challenged patient who was never quiet. All day long he delivered his concert of loud laughter, shouts, whistles and snatches of songs. One day I pointed him out, "Your majesty, (this was his favourite form of address, although he also accepted Messiah, King, God or, even, Your Highness) why is that subject behaving in that manner?" He studied the subject for a time before he answered, "The difficulty with that subject is that he neglected to commence." Not a bad diagnosis when one thinks of it, although an ordinary person might have said something like, "He got off to a bad start."

My phone awakened me once after midnight. It was Bill. He had come off the afternoon shift and couldn't wait to share with me the Messiah's latest. He had approached the Messiah and gone into a spiel, "Your Majesty, we have a subject in prison who is a scoundrel. He won't work. His children are starving. He beats his wife," and so on in that vein. The Messiah's decision came quickly, "This calls for the judicial use of the hemp."

McGregor was not our only Christ returned. Dr. Ehrlich, who had apparently taken the time to look into this, told our class that we had more than twenty assorted saviours, messiahs and redeemers among our population. On one occasion he brought a fairly recent admission to our class for a clinical demonstration. His family had reported him behaving strangely, and intimating that he was the returned Christ. The patient was suspicious and reluctant to communicate. He denied vehemently that he was Christ. The doctor would leave the topic for a while, then return to it after a few innocuous questions. His technique was very skillful. The patient finally became indignant, "OK, so I am Jesus. What are you going to do about it?" This patient was discharged not long after, and we never saw him again. It is probable that his delusions were not too deeply seated or, possibly, his family accepted him as he was; at least he would not be a threat to anyone.

One day Dr. Coulter came out of a patient interview with a smile on his face, "It looks like we might have a second-generation Jesus here."

Alec Tatarin might be considered a "hail fellow well met" kind of Jesus. He didn't demand any kind of obsequiousness, didn't mind being called by his name. He was always of good humour, smiling and sociable. A handsome man who sported a well-trimmed moustache, he was always natty and well turned-out. Wearing his nice checked windbreaker and wide-brimmed fedora he walked about the grounds lifting his hat to the ladies and bestowing cheerful greetings all around. He knew that when the call came he would do what was ordained; but until then he was content with life as it was.

It was his son who had also been admitted with the delusion that he was Jesus. A small, meek twenty-year-old, he gave the impression of being frightened and lost in his new surroundings. I knew that Alec had been brought over to Admission to visit with his son, so the next time I saw him I said, "Hey, Alec. You've been over to see the boy. How's he doing?"

"Oh, he's crazy as hell," he guffawed. "He thinks he's Jesus."

Among our group of four we imagined how that meeting might have gone:

Alec: Why are you here?

Son: They brought me here because I said I was Jesus.

Alec: You can't be Jesus. I'm Jesus.

Son: Can't I be Jesus too?

Alec: Don't be stupid. Get home and help your mother on the farm.

It is quite possible that while visiting his father during his impressionable years, the seeds of his delusion were planted in his mind. As a deeply religious, impressionable youth (or as we were taught, pre-disposed) his father's claim to the most exalted position must have left a mark. At any rate, he was not with us long, a few ECT's and a period of socialization and he was gone and, apparently, cured. At least he was never re-admitted during the time I was there.

At that time the "Returned Christ" was one of the most common delusions in Canadian mental hospitals. In literature the classic delusion is usually Napoleon or some other king or emperor. That may still be true in Europe, but I never met a single patient who believed himself to be a "Royal". We had one man who claimed that he was the legitimate husband of the Queen, and that Prince Philip was an imposter, a usurper. However, he was not very serious about it. He would talk about this injustice without anger, in fact, with an accepting and philosophical air, as though he knew that it was only a matter of time before the situation was rectified.

Chapter 19

Something a Man Couldn't Do

The notion that a human being could believe himself to be a member of a different species is the stuff of barroom jokes and comic strips. Yet in SHNB we actually had two patients who had the delusion that they were of the equine race.

On the male side we had Jim Fielding, another patient for whom I developed a real affection. Looking in his file, I found that when he was admitted during the thirties he was diagnosed with schizophrenia, hebephrenic type. We all believed that this diagnosis was incorrect. Hebephrenics withdraw into a fantasy world where things are pleasant and pleasurable. They are often seen displaying strange mannerisms, and laughing inappropriately. To have any kind of conversation with a chronic hebephrenic is usually not possible.

Jim, on the contrary, was very bright, very focused. He knew what a horse should be and worked hard at getting it right. He had trained his lower lip to hang down, and often bobbed his head up and down with teeth bared, as horses are wont to do. As he moved about he might display a purposeful walk, a trot, or a high-stepping gait. He was even a bit smelly, the way a horse should be.

You never saw him without a straw, or a stem of grass, hanging from his mouth. This was no problem in the summer when the patients were taken out to enjoy the fresh air, but during the winter months he would have to resort to a straw from the broom.

He would often trot up to where the staff were posted and stand there expectantly. We knew that he wanted to be given some work to do. Most of the time we had nothing to offer him. "We don't need you right now, Jim," we would say, and he would trot away to sit down and wait for his favourite time of day.

This came always on the afternoon shift. At some point would come the call "Blocks, boys!" This would be the signal for certain patients, with Jim in the lead, to go to the "block room" and bring out a "block".

The blocks were simply that, heavy blocks of wood to which brushes had been attached. They had been manufactured there, in the hospital's occupational therapy department (sometimes called the toy shop). Their purpose was twofold: to give a shine to the ward floor and, at the same time, provide some physical activity for the patients.

It was interesting and revealing to watch various patients as they engaged in this work. Most simply walked in the same circle, while others would walk up and down, polishing the same line. There were a few, however, who sought out areas needing extra buffing, or who worked the corners, demonstrating that, at one time they were reliable and capable workers.

For Jim, it was, quite literally, his moment to shine and he took full advantage of it. He would vary his gaits. Pretending to be spooked by something, he would shy sideways, emitting a loud snort. Occasionally, he would break into a gallop, causing his block to swing dangerously outward. We would have to intervene, "Whoa, whoa, Jim, slow down!"

While the polishing was going on the staff table and chairs were put out of the way into a side-room. After the blocks were put away someone would call, "Chairs, Jim."

High stepping all the while, Jim would bring each item of furniture and set it in its place. The task completed, he would snort, and make the utterance we waited for, "That's something a man couldn't do." For our gang of four it became a sort of a mantra, something we would repeat after completing anything requiring some effort, "something a man couldn't do". Our wives probably got thoroughly sick of it.

    During the months of summer we took our patients out for walks on practically a daily basis. Jim would always trail the group. He would be set on a "plod" and it was something to see, the way he had it down so perfectly. Quite frequently we would meet a group from the female side – which included the other horse, who was called Johnny. Johnny also liked to trail behind the group where she would trot in a zig-zag pattern, neighing constantly. We noticed that Jim always seemed to study her at length. Some staff thought it was a sexual interest, but I did not agree. I always thought that he was just offended by her un-horselike behaviour.

    A quarter of a century later I found Jim gone; the blocks too were gone to "block heaven". In their place was a paid house-keeping staff with electric polishers. Johnny was gone too. I consider myself very lucky to have known Jim. His like will not be seen again.

Chapter 20

Disgusting Creatures

  I arrived on 10B one hot summer day for the afternoon shift. After the change of shift formalities were over I noticed that there was something different in the way Tony Wozniak was behaving. It was not that his mannerisms were unusual; it was more that they seemed exaggerated. Tony had a claim to fame in that years before, when he had grounds privileges he had attempted to castrate himself using the lid of an open tin can that he had found. He was one of several on the ward who never sat down except at meal times. His usual position was to lean on the wall near the staff station with his eyes tightly closed. Every few moments he would give his body a jerk, at the same time emitting a sound something like "pshaw". But that day he was repeating this mannerism more frequently, and his vocalization seemed louder. It would have been reasonable to assume that he was becoming disturbed, going "up the pole" in our vernacular, except that Tony was considered stable; he had no reputation of becoming disturbed. He appeared flushed, but his temperature was only slightly above normal.

  "Hold the fort, guys," I said. "I'm taking Tony to 2B, let the doc have a look at him."

  While waiting for the duty doctor to arrive, we charted his pulse, temperature and respiration. The Turkish doctor came in, had a look in his mouth, then moved to his right ear. He made an exclamation, and reeled back, "There are animals in there!" We all had a look, and sure enough, his ear was teeming with white squirming maggots. His left ear was normal. His ear was immediately washed out and, at the end, the kidney basin seemed to contain hundreds of the disgusting creatures. Some of the staff were having a hard time keeping their last meal down and, even I, who could deal with a pool of diarrhea and go straight to lunch, was feeling a bit queasy.

It didn't bother me too much, however, for there was a time when I worked closely with maggots, even went out of my way to make sure they were healthy and comfortable.

It is common knowledge that maggots have been used in medicine to clean out gangrenous tissue but, in my time in New Zealand, I discovered another area where man put maggots to work to his advantage.

It was in the summer of 1949 that I worked in the village of Pareora, in the South Island of New Zealand. Pareora was Clara's hometown, and we rented half the house from Clara's parents, my in-laws. In that little village was found a "freezing works", where, during a few months of seasonal work I made the best money I ever had to that point.

It was an amazingly efficient enterprise. Six thousand lambs were dispatched there daily, and no part of them was wasted. Between meat, wool, skins, tallow, sausage casings, fertilizer and chicken feed, every part of the animal was used.

My job was in the skins department. After the skins were washed and put through a dryer, they came down a moving table where a corrosive paint was applied to the skin side. Next day the wool could simply be wiped off; that is how "lambs-wool" from which expensive sweaters are made is obtained.

However, in the skinning of the animal there were "trimmings", little pieces of skin from around the legs and ears, which were too small and "finicky" for painting, and were simply trimmed off. Yet each little piece of skin contained a few strands of wool, too valuable to waste.

Probably the solution was discovered by accident. Someone noted that where a pile of trimmings had been infested with maggots, the wool pulled off easily.

So the thousands of trimmings were laid out on a large cemented area in fields about a foot thick, called (what else?) "pies", and flies were invited to come and do what they do best. In a few days the "pies" were teeming with maggots.

However, it could not be left at that. The maggots had to be cared for, protected. As I was always willing to work all the hours I could get, that became my weekend job at a good overtime rate.

The problem was that if the pie was too thick it would get overheated, and the maggots would die. When a certain temperature was reached it was necessary to spread the pies out and that was my responsibility.

Fortunately, I did not develop any great affection for the maggots, for they were not allowed to live out their life span. As soon as they had done their work loosening the fibres on the scraps of lambskin, the pies were put through a bath of boiling water and the appetizing aroma of boiled maggots would permeate the village. The pie-men would then, by hand, pull out the strands of wool. This was called "pie-wool", the most valuable of all.

And at the outfall where the tasty morsels, along with blood and other offal, were washed into the Pacific lurked fish and other sea creatures waiting to be fed. It was a favourite fishing spot for Pareora people, and you had to be pretty inept to come home without a catch of some kind.

No Ordinary Job

I had heard talk about a monster conger eel which had been seen there, and it seemed to be the ambition of local fishermen to be the one to catch it. It turned out that the lucky one was my father-in-law. He came home with the eel draped over his shoulder, and it was so long that the tail dragged behind him on the ground. It was as thick as a man's leg. So we had eel every meal that day and the next, but most of it was taken to my Maori brother-in-law, Ken Rangi, for smoking. It was not common in those days for people to have a refrigerator, much less a freezer. As for smoked conger, it must be one of the foods of the gods.

Poor Tony, he of course, lost hearing in the infested ear, the maggots having done a good job of cleaning out most of the soft tissue. Incredibly, the following summer he had another infestation in the same ear. It was often noted that when he was out relaxing in a grassy area, he would lie on his right side with his head on the ground. An opportunistic fly obviously considered his ear an ideal place to raise a family. After that it became our habit to check his ears periodically. So far as I knew, they remained "maggot-free".

Chapter 21

Is That Clock Right?

I had a group from 4B, the insulin shock ward, out for a walk one afternoon when I noticed Dan McMahon standing off to the side, gazing into the distance. He was in his customary grey suit and fedora, leaning on his cane. The cane was not an affectation; he was a wounded veteran of The Great War, and walked with a pronounced limp. This did not prevent him from being a rover. A popular figure, he pretty well had open access to all areas of the hospital. He liked to walk around visiting various wards, chatting, accepting cups of tea and snacks. He had gotten to know a good number of patients and had his favourites. He always made a point of discussing the state of the realm with Messiah, God King, and would join René Roberge in a song. With new staff he liked to put on an act, pretending that he was really "out of it". I heard him once in conversation with a couple of young female students, "I own this house. I rented this house to you and I don't see a garden anywhere around this house." Another time, pointing to a patient sitting in his bed he asked, "What time is it by that clock?"

Anyway, there he was, and I stopped the group to have a talk with him. I always had a warm spot for him since he was the first person I saw when I came to apply for a job some years before. Also, of late, he seemed to have changed his habits. As long as anyone could remember he spent a good part of most afternoons at what we called the "front office", the reception area. There, he would read the paper and go through numerous cigarettes. As a result, when he stopped appearing there, it was noticed. The receptionist spoke to me about it one day, "I haven't seen Dan for quite a while. Is he OK?"

No Ordinary Job

So, after the usual greetings, I brought it up. "Say, Dan, how come you're not hanging around the front office any more?"

He sort of chuckled, "I'll tell you what happened."

It seems he was lying in bed one night when he thought of a good joke. It was then he began to spend his afternoons, the usual visiting hours, in the reception area. It took eight years before someone fed him the line he needed, "Is that clock right?" and he was finally able to reply, "If that clock was right, it wouldn't be here."

That was it, the joke that had governed his afternoons all those years. For those of us "in the know" it was a good joke, but whether it was worth waiting eight years for the punch line is debatable.

"I can't begin to tell you how many people asked 'Is that the right time?' but that wouldn't work," Dan elaborated.

Actually, the thought behind his joke could apply to Dan himself. We could not understand why he had been there for all those years. As far as everyone was concerned he was "right", there was nothing wrong with him. I never did see his file. Since the parole building was often unsupervised patient files were not available for perusal. Some older staff seemed to remember a problem with alcohol. He must have had family somewhere, yet no one could remember him having a visitor.

The only thing that might suggest that he belonged there was the fact that he seemed so contented with the situation. He never "eloped" or tried to obtain his discharge.

It was Jimmy Chrysler who put it into perspective one day.

"Where could he have it better? He gets everything he needs here. He's got the run of the place. His pension goes into his account; he can buy all the tailor-mades and peppermints he wants. Joe Wilks (the patient who did the drycleaning) cleans his suit for free. Would he be better off renting a room somewhere, or stuck in some old-folks home?"

Not at all. Dan had figured out that he was on to a pretty good thing; there were probably quite a few others like him.

Chapter 22

Leave That Up To the Old Man

Although everyone knew that Irrigation 3 was a busy ward staff were generally happy to be rotated to it. It was in a new wing that had been built for geriatric patients. This was another well-run ward where staff went that extra mile. And it was all to the patients' benefit. I have seen geriatric wards in other provinces and also extended care units attached to general hospitals. Some were much inferior to Irrigation 3, with beds crowded together and patients parked in dayrooms for endless hours. The ward had a couple dozen ambulant patients who looked after themselves well and had a comfortable dayroom to themselves.

A quasi sick-ward, the majority were bed patients although many of these were ambulant. Each patient had a gatch-frame bed that could be adjusted for comfort. Patients breakfasted in bed; during the day they might sit in their beds or in comfortable chairs. Any sign of discomfort or of fatigue and they could be down again. Any bed-sore was immediately treated and in that ward pressure sores were non-existent. If patients became ill, they were not transferred out, they were treated in the ward until they recovered or...

So, it was a satisfying place to work. It is natural for workers in any profession to want to see results for what they do. Another reason for my liking the ward was Pat Gally. Often it happened that another of our "gang of four" was on the ward at the same time. We all had a great affection for Pat, as we did for any patient who showed character traits out of the ordinary. We had been told that he was a living link with the Wild West, with Billy the Kid and such like, and since he was in his nineties it was possible. He endeared himself to us by the quality of his profane vocabulary and we could not resist aggravating him to the point where he was in full flight, and it didn't take much. My favourite Pat quotation was "You're so god damned ignorant you couldn't pour piss out of a boot if the directions were written on the sole." Of course the words were interspersed with a good sprinkling of "f's". If we found him with a wet bed or worse, we would invariably say, "Hey, Pat, that bloody whore you dragged in here last night pissed your bed again. Oh, Christ, she crapped your bed too." This would bring on a string of profanities beyond belief, but when you looked at his face you could see he was being forced to remember what had happened. "I paid for this room and I can do whatever I f'ing want." Once I said to him, "Pat, you should look for some nice women. Your women always piss your bed." To which he had a good answer, "You couldn't even get a sheep to stand still for you."

  We noticed that every time Pat got really fired up he would go scrabbing under his pillow. "I bet he's looking for a gun!" Maurice exclaimed. He took it upon himself to obtain a realistic looking pistol. Chrome plated, it fired disc caps rather than half caps. After slipping it under Pat's pillow we went through the usual routine at bed check. Sure enough, when he reached the boiling point, Pat reached under his pillow and found the weapon. The joy on his face was something to behold. The way he fired the gun showed he had experience – he raised it, then brought it down to eye-level, aimed and fired. Staff were falling "dead" all over the place.

  Yes, we were amusing ourselves at the patients' expense, guilty as charged. Do I feel bad about it? Not a bit. The majority of old patients lay quietly in their beds, and lived out their time well cared for and that's all. We like to think that the stimulation Pat received as a reward for his special talent added years to his life. At any rate, he was still going strong when I left the place.

Peter Kline, who inhabited the same ward, was another "Christ returned". Unlike the Messiah, God King, he did not pretend to be the ruler of the world. He was satisfied with being the returned Christ. Still he demanded all the respect that was due to him. Nevertheless, it was possible to sit beside him and discuss a variety of subjects. Although of German origin, he knew Russian and I could go to him for a bit of conversation practice.

Although he was nowhere near as amusing as Messiah, God King he endeared himself to us in his own way. On the 25th of December he would announce to all "It's my birthday today." Even staff working on other wards would bring him gifts. Nothing fancy needed: some crackers and a tin of sardines or some snoose, which he used copiously but fastidiously. At times we would have some women's group or possibly, a conscientious clergyman visit the ward. Frequently they would ask for the names of a few patients so they could greet them by name. They would approach Peter with big smiles, "And how are you, Mr. Kline?" His response was always "I'm not Mr. Kline. I'm your God."

The winter of 1955-56 is said to have been the most severe in Saskatchewan history. One blizzard followed another with intense cold temperatures. Several people caught in blizzards perished on the roads, including an RCMP officer from North Battleford. Cattle froze standing in the fields. Farmers blinded by the wind-blown snow would go astray between the house and the barn and perish within yards of their home. There were three occasions when the relieving staff could not get to the hospital and staff on duty had to work around the clock.

It was on one of those occasions when something happened which recompensed me for all the downsides of the job. Irrigation 3 was a very nice ward with wide corridors and floor-to-ceiling windows. It was early morning and we were waiting for breakfast to come up. We had been there on shift for more than twenty-four hours, taking turns to snatch a couple of hours sleep. I was standing beside Peter's chair, looking out one of those big windows. All that could be seen was a curtain of white blowing snow. "Hey, Jesus," I said, "why don't you do something about this weather?" The answer came instantly. "Oh, the weather, I leave that up to the old man."

He couldn't realize that right there he had made it all worthwhile for me – the low wages, the smells, the unpleasant tasks, the cold drives, the interminable night shifts – all compensated for in a moment.

Afterword

For the last few years of his life, my dad, Ed Skalazub, carried around a blue cloth bag containing his "book". After much contemplation he had begun to write down his memories of his time at SHNB during a trip to Cuba with his second wife, Winnie. These memories were, in many cases, dad's stories, which he told at the dinner table or on visits with friends and relatives. Often, listeners would respond with "You've got to write a book about this." And so, he did. When dad was struck by the illness that would kill him, in the spring of 2011, he took his much-travelled book bag with him to the hospital, and when he passed I made sure to take the bag home with me, aware of its precious contents. A year and a half went by before I began to pull together the pieces of dad's book. Many sections had been re-written into a large blue ledger book. Some notes existed as rough drafts in coil notebooks, others on random sheets of paper. In organizing, editing and formatting the pages I received from dad I did my best to preserve his original intent while respecting chronology and coherence. I know dad checked many of his facts with his lifelong friend Maurice Anderson and he deserves mention and thanks. It was dad's intent to provide a picture of "what it was like" to work in a psychiatric hospital in Saskatchewan in the 1950's. I hope the vividness of his experience and his fondness for the patients shine through in this memoir, as they always did when he told these stories. For those unfamiliar with dad's biography, following the period described in this memoir our family moved to B.C. in 1961. After graduation from UBC in 1965 he began a 20-year career as a high school French teacher at Maple Ridge Secondary. But that, as they say, is another story.

Allan Skalazub,   March, 2013

Made in the USA
Lexington, KY
01 December 2019